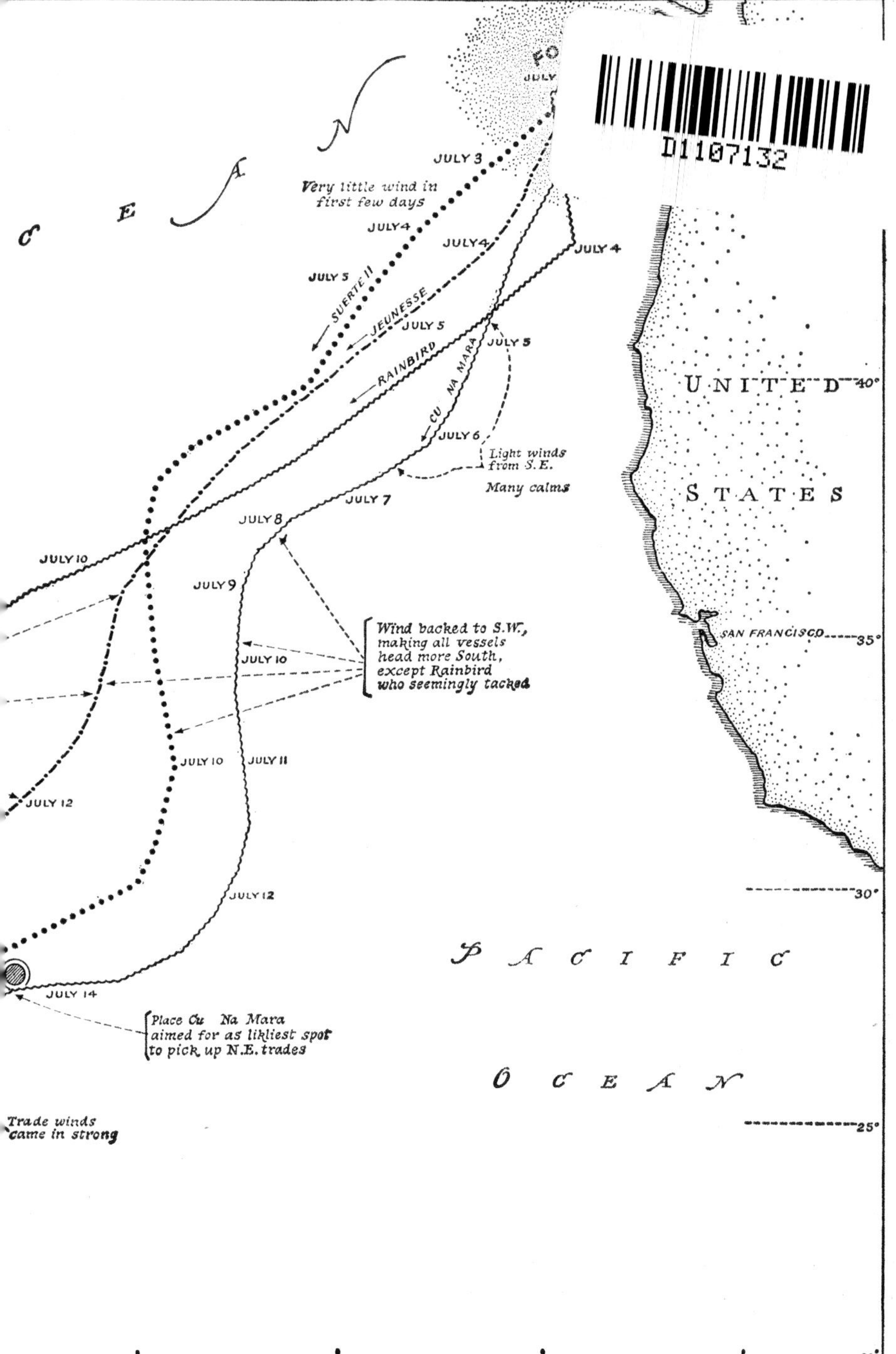
C E A N
JULY 3
Very little wind in first few days
JULY 4
JULY 4
JULY 4
JULY 5
SUERTE II
JEUNESSE
JULY 5
RAINBIRD
JULY 5
CU NA MARA
JULY 6
Light winds from S.E.
Many calms
JULY 7
JULY 8
JULY 10
JULY 9
Wind backed to S.W., making all vessels head more South, except Rainbird who seemingly tacked
JULY 10
JULY 10
JULY 11
JULY 12
JULY 12
JULY 14
Place Cu Na Mara aimed for as likliest spot to pick up N.E. trades
Trade winds came in strong
UNITED STATES
SAN FRANCISCO
40°
35°
30°
25°
20°
PACIFIC OCEAN
135°
130°
125°
120°

*Hound of the Sea*

Other Books by LEONARD WIBBERLEY

ADVENTURES OF AN ELEPHANT BOY

THE ROAD FROM TOOMI

FEAST OF FREEDOM

THE ISLAND OF THE ANGELS

THE MOUSE ON THE MOON

THE MOUSE THAT ROARED

STRANGER AT KILLKNOCK

THE HANDS OF CORMAC JOYCE

TAKE ME TO YOUR PRESIDENT

BEWARE OF THE MOUSE

NO GARLIC IN THE SOUP!

THE QUEST OF EXCALIBUR

THE LAND THAT ISN'T THERE

YESTERDAY'S LAND

VENTURES INTO THE DEEP

THE TIME OF THE LAMB

BALLAD OF THE PILGRIM CAT

THE SHEPHERD'S REWARD

FIJI: ISLANDS OF THE DAWN

TOWARD A DISTANT ISLAND

SOMETHING TO READ

# *Hound of the Sea*

by

LEONARD WIBBERLEY

IVES WASHBURN, INC.
New York

HOUND OF THE SEA



Library of Congress Catalog Card Number: 69-19955

MANUFACTURED IN THE UNITED STATES OF AMERICA

VAN REES PRESS • NEW YORK

*Hound of the Sea*

# Chapter One

SOME YEARS AGO, while at sea, I was seized by a fit of madness which drove me to decide to engage in an ocean race. What brought this about was the great weight of the wind which I was experiencing at that time and the tremendous speed which my forty-foot yawl, *Bahia,* was achieving. For although she was but a cruising boat, and, again, although she had up only working sail, *Bahia* in one day on that particular voyage reeled over two hundred miles in twenty-four hours, and the next day almost equaled that performance with one hundred and eighty miles. In three days she made a run of five hundred and sixty miles, and that is a performance quite up to the standard of ocean racers—and beyond the achievement of many of them.

And so madness overtook me and, deeply enamoured of my boat, I decided that I would enter *Bahia* in an ocean race and the ocean race I would enter her in would be the Transpacific Yacht Race, called, for short, the Transpac.

This is a convenient ocean race for me, for it starts just

outside San Pedro, California, which is not much more than a dozen miles from my home in Hermosa Beach.

The course, if that is the term, is a trifle over two thousand miles and the finish is in Honolulu, Hawaii, where I had already taken *Bahia.* In fact, it was on the voyage back from Honolulu that she showed such astonishing speed and so stimulated me to insanity.

I will not now go into the full details of how, returning to California, I immediately set about preparing *Bahia* for the Transpac—which was the equivalent of preparing the family car for the Indianapolis, though I did not know this at that time. In fact, at that time I knew nothing whatever about ocean racing and presumed that an ocean race was a simple matter of getting your boat to a certain starting line at a certain time and belting it as hard as you could to a finish line some distance off. That concept is, I believe, shared by thousands of my fellow yachtsmen who will profit, then, by reading what follows.

For I soon found that to enter an ocean race required the expenditure of enormous sums of money and a prodigious amount of labor; that in fact it is almost impossible to enter an ocean race without several thousand dollars at your disposal and a secretariat rivaling that of the United Nations in time of crisis. A few new sails, I thought, a little lightening of my gear here and there, and the dumping overboard of unnecessary stores should put me in racing trim. But I found that *Bahia* had also to be weighed and measured and certificated by a Cruising Club of America measurer, and equipped with items like man-overboard-poles with slabs of shark repellent attached to them, and life jackets (also with shark repellent and sea dye) and lifelines and self-igniting lights and a score of other things (all necessary beyond a doubt) so that months and large sums of money were spent in preparing *Bahia*. And when it was all done, she was rejected by the selection committee which ruled on which yacht could, or could not, enter the race.

*Bahia* was rejected for good reasons. I cannot quarrel with them. She was a cruising boat, not a racing boat. She was gaff-rigged on her main, and thus old-fashioned, not modern. And there was a huge entry of modern racing yachts some of whom had to be turned away. The committee could not accept *Bahia* with her old-fashioned gaff and topsail rig and turn down boats of later and faster design.

And so *Bahia* was rejected, and my madness had borne its first fruits of frustration. But this did not cure the madness.

For the reason that they all looked alike, I have never become greatly interested in modern racing sloops with what is called a masthead rig—that is, with the headsails going up to the topmost point of the mast. Surely, part of the pleasure of possession is to have something different from what others have. I do not like possessions of which everyone else has an exact copy. Furthermore, I distrusted, out of pure prejudice, boats built of fiberglass. It seemed to me pathetic that such boats were always advertised as having "genuine teak (or mahogany) trim" or "lavish use of teak throughout," as if they knew that they should really be made of wood and were trying their best to atone for the fact that they weren't.

*Bahia* had inch-and-a-half Douglas fir planking, and, in touching a reef going into the Ala Wai Yacht Harbor near Honolulu,* had stove three planks. What would have happened, I wondered, had she been made of fiberglass? She would surely have cracked open like an egg.

* See *Toward a Distant Island.*

One day my son Kevin, eighteen, announced he was going to an international surfing contest at nearby Huntington Beach and I went with him. The contest is held each year on both sides of the Huntington Beach Pier, which thus provides a huge grandstand for spectators. There was a heavy south swell the day of the contest and a number of surfers lost their boards which were taken ashore by the waves, slamming into every concrete piling of the pier on the way. Now, surfboards are of polyurethane foam which is pretty soft, covered by a couple of layers of fiberglass. And I looked at some of those boards when they reached the beach. They had welts and dents in them all right. But none of them had been splintered or broken in half, as would certainly have happened had they been made of wood.

That was a pretty impressive display and I wondered whether I was misjudging fiberglass. My friend, Miles Davidson, owned a Columbia 28, *Pirouette,* and he invited me to come aboard one day and look her over. I was impressed by the amount of room aboard and when he lifted up the floorboards and showed me the bilges with just a drop of pure clear water in them I began to have more liberal views on the subject of fiberglass hulls.

Then Kevin started to talk about sailing modern fiberglass sloops. He had crewed on a few of them. The winches were great, he said. You could trim a really big Genoa to a fraction with practically no effort. Getting up the main was no worry. If we had a fiberglass boat of say thirty-four feet with a masthead rig and aluminum spars, he said, the two of us could easily handle it and enter all the races we wanted. Maybe if we got it in time, we could even enter the Transpac that year—the race for which *Bahia* had been rejected.

The word Transpac conquered all. My insanity possessed

me again and in full force. Certainly, I decided, *Bahia* must be sold, a new and modern boat bought, and the Transpac entered.

"This time," I assured my wife Hazel and the rest of my family, "there are going to be no snap decisions. We are going to look over every kind of yacht that is available for the price we can afford to pay. We are going to compare prices and qualities and do everything in a sensible and deliberate fashion; proving that millions of years of man's evolution have put him in control of his emotions."

I don't know why I said all that because it wasn't in the slightest degree true. I had already decided that I was going to buy a Morgan 34 from seeing one in the advertisements in yachting magazines. It looked different from the other thirty-four-foot racing sloops and that is why I decided to buy it. Still, it made me feel sensible to talk about shopping about, as if I were capable of doing things in a rational manner—which in my case is utterly untrue.

However, these little deceits console us and I actually did look at two other boats before going down to Joe Stephen's agency in Newport Beach to find out about the Morgan 34. I looked at a very elegant and narrow sloop, about forty feet long and as deep as a coffin, which a lady wanted to sell. But I didn't like it. It was so narrow I had the feeling I would have to go forward along the deck sideways. I looked at a thirty-seven-foot fiberglass sloop which also was going cheap. She looked like a very fast boat, but the belowdecks smelled abominably of some kind of chemical which I suspected would flavor everything aboard for years.

My duty to rational shopping done, I rushed over to the Stephens Agency to find out about the Morgan whose picture had taken my fancy in the magazines. The design looked different from others of the same kind. There was a slight tumble home amidships producing a pleasing line. There was a graceful sheer, and there was one further attractive feature—at that time there was only one other Morgan 34 in the whole of Southern California. With any luck, I could spend years sailing mine and never come across the other guy.

I was introduced at the agency to Jerry Malmburg who had been aboard *Escudero,* a Columbia design (but by Charles Morgan who had designed the Morgan 34), in a previous Transpac. She had been well up in the fleet when she lost her mast. Jerry was pleasant, obliging, cheerful, and took us aboard the other Morgan. She was called *Black Baron,* had a jet black hull, and looked lovely. We went over her very carefully and in the sparkling sun with the lovely blue water around and the homes of the wealthy on every hand, concluded that everyone ought to have a home in Newport Beach with a slip right in front of his house and a yacht moored to the slip.

Newport Beach has an atmosphere of entrancing luxury about it. This atmosphere makes you feel much richer than you are and entitled by right to a share of the very best things on earth. Newport Beach is rather like a Rolls Royce—once you get inside you wonder what on earth you have been doing in all those cheap cars for so long. I was aware of these effects of Newport Beach before I went there and determined to steel myself against them. I reminded myself that I came from Hermosa Beach, which isn't in the slightest degree fashionable, and lived in a frame house with a great number of termites who have spent the last three years trying to remove my living room window. I told myself that I was just a working author and if I committed myself to the purchase of a yacht of the quality of a Morgan

34, I would spend the next several years in anguish trying to make the payments. I certainly assured myself sternly that there could be no question of buying one boat while I still owned another.

So when we had looked over *Black Baron*—the black walnut built-ins below with her teak and holly cabin floor and her luxurious cushions and fittings—I collected a number of brochures from Jerry about the Morgan 34, bid him a cordial farewell, and said I would let him know in a little while whether I wanted a boat or not. And he mentioned that there was one nearing completion which he thought I could have and which would certainly be delivered, if that was my wish, in time for the Transpac.

Then we went to one of those Newport Beach restaurants whose customers all seem to be living happily on a hundred thousand dollars a year. Across the road was a view of the bay and tied up at a slip was an elegant yacht on which a blue and gold drifter was being raised to dry. Kevin was with me and Hazel, too, and I repeated my formula about being sensible and not rushing into anything. I mentioned that there would be many Transpacs and we didn't have to get into the one immediately ahead.

We had sensible coffee and sandwiches instead of pheasant under glass, which I think was available, and I marveled at the serenity of the blue and gold drifter filling in the light harbor breeze. Then I collected the bill and Hazel said: "What are you going to call her?"

*"Cu Na Mara,"* I said. "It means Hound of the Sea." And I went back to Jerry to order the Morgan 34.

# *Chapter Two*

WHEN YOU ORDER a new yacht these days, what you get is something that will float but will not, in the condition in which it is delivered, sail. In other words, sails do not come with sailboats. They are extra and they are only one of many extras which you will find yourself buying with many yachts, while the bill mounts and mounts.

In this respect, I have to state immediately that the Morgan was far more complete than many other yachts. She had her masts with their rigging, her boom with its roller reefing gear (and very good gear, too), all her basic winches and full lifelines, as well as a pulpit or railing around the bow and what is whimsically called a pushpit or railing around the stern. Nothing whatever had to be added below decks. The bunks were in and the cushions were there, too—nice thick, firm ones covered in black Naugahyde and very well tailored. I ordered my yacht (perhaps under the influence of that luxurious Newport Beach atmosphere) with genuine black walnut trim below and formica panelling of black walnut pattern to match. Her cabin floor was of teak with white holly strips laid between each plank, and very fetching indeed. The little companionway stairway from the cockpit to belowdecks was of black walnut and all this wood, quite lavish really, was polished but unvarnished. The extras I had to buy, or decided to buy, were very few compared with what is usually the case. Since the boat was to be readied for the Transpac, I ordered two spinnaker poles (one hundred and fifty dollars each) and an extra twenty-five-gallon stainless steel water tank (to bring my total capacity in tanks to fifty gallons) and an extra gasoline tank (again bringing the capacity to fifty gallons) for the reason that after the Transpac I proposed to do some exploring around the Hawaiian Islands and would use the engine extensively.

I don't like tillers except on small boats and for short passages and so I ordered a wheel for *Cu Na Mara,* which cost a trifle over a thousand dollars extra. Also, rigging rollers to prevent the Genoa chafing on the shrouds. Also, a three-bladed propellor (for the exploring around the Islands—the tide runs hard through the gaps in the reefs and you need a big prop to push against it) and an insulated backstay as an antenna for my radiotelephone. I thought I did well with the extras. There was, roughly, only about sixteen hundred dollars spent on them. And then came the one big extra which I had somehow overlooked.

It would cost me fifteen hundred dollars, I discovered, just to have the boat shipped to me! The Morgan shipyard is in Florida and the price of the boat did not include the cost of getting it to me. The base price, as it is called, was nineteen thousand dollars. Add fifteen hundred dollars for shipment. Add sixteen hundred dollars for extras. Add fifteen hundred dollars for a Genoa, a mainsail and a spinnaker. Add one hundred and thirty dollars for the cradle the boat was shipped on. And don't forget sales tax. Would you have settled for twenty-four thousand dollars? That is about what I settled for when I got my yacht in the water and ready to sail. The moral, or part of it, is—when buying a boat buy one that is manufactured locally so as to avoid those big shipping costs which must come on top of the base price.

A month, at the most, it was thought, would see *Cu Na Mara* in our hands and so I wrote to England for the sails and was assured that I would have them in four weeks time if I would authorize delivery by air mail. This I authorized without a qualm because having spent twenty-four thousand dollars for the boat, I was not about to quarrel over postage stamps. By the way, that twenty-four thousand for a generously equipped boat is a very good bargain. I can remember the time when a thirty-four-foot boat would have cost thirty-four thousand dollars—for in wood the price used to be about one thousand dollars per foot of length. Fiberglass construction is bringing down the price of boats fast and making yachting available to many who previously could not afford it.

Meanwhile, Joe Stephens, who runs the Stephens Agency, found a buyer for *Bahia* at a reasonable price, so that was off my mind—though I parted with her with anguish. I was able to make a substantial deposit on *Cu Na Mara* and borrow the rest from my bank. And then I called up Mr. Gordon Curtis, secretary of the Transpac Committee, who had had the unpleasant task of rejecting my previous entry, and told him I had a new boat, a thirty-four-foot sloop, which I wished to enter in the Transpac and I hoped there was still room.

He was sincerely happy about the whole thing. He asked

me the name of the boat and some of her dimensions and the name of the designer. I said I hadn't got a C.C.A. (Cruising Club of America) rating for her but would get one as soon as she arrived. He said he would see me at the starting line. Just that sentence was almost worth the whole twenty-four thousand dollars so anxious was I now to get into an ocean race. I rejoiced in the thought that I was finally going to make it. I had prepared one boat and I had bought another and now I was to be able to race.

But it just was not to be. A little later Mr. Curtis called me back and he sounded depressed. What did I say was *Cu Na Mara*'s waterline, he asked.

"Right around twenty-four feet, six inches," I said.

There was one of those horrible pauses when the air begins to feel heavy and the walls of houses sag. "I'm afraid she isn't going to make it," said Mr. Curtis slowly. "I have been inquiring about the design and she will be too small on the L, I believe."

He explained what the L was. It is a theoretical waterline obtained by taking .3 of the actual waterline and adding it to .7 of the distance measured along the hull four per cent above the actual waterline. That figure, to qualify for the Transpac, had to come out to thirty feet. *Cu Na Mara,* he thought, would come out almost three feet short. Didn't the Morgan Company make a yacht a foot or two longer. Or wouldn't it be possible for me to get a boat that was a foot or two longer?

It wasn't. *Cu Na Mara* was bought and signed for. She had already been shipped from Florida. For the Transpac, I had bought the wrong boat—she just wouldn't qualify.

I don't suppose many have made two such blunders; fitted out a boat for a race at enormous expense only to have it rejected as insufficiently modern. And then bought another for the same race only to have it rejected as the wrong size. What was particularly aggravating was that the first boat I had looked at and which I had turned down because of the chemical smell aboard, would have qualified and would have cost less than *Cu Na Mara.*

I adjusted to the situation by deciding that I was going to race to Hawaii anyway. I couldn't race officially, but I could start when the Transpac fleet started and see how well I could do against the other contenders. There was no need, now, to get a Cruising Club of America certificate (essential for ocean racing) which saved me eighty dollars. *Cu Na Mara* would be the smallest boat making the distance so if she beat anybody at all she would be doing pretty well. The next nearest size was a Cal 36, and beyond that came the Cal 40s.

As I have said, when I learned that *Cu Na Mara* was too small she was already on her way, somewhere between Florida and California. When she arrived, she surprised me. The hull profile I had been shown had an attached rudder—that is to say a rudder right behind the keel and strapped to it by gudgeons and pintles. But *Cu Na Mara* had a spade rudder—a rudder separate from the keel, moved back under her counter. I had some doubts about it immediately. Spade rudders are designed to give more control over a boat, particularly when running downwind which is the most dangerous point of sailing. But I knew of boats which had lost spade rudders because the strain on them is tremendous.

In effect, the rudder is asked to do a considerable part of the work of the keel, which is reduced in size to a fin and thus has a reduced ability to keep the boat heading straight on its course. The work the fin cannot do is handed over to the rudder. Being moved aft, the rudder has, of course, more leverage over the whole length of the boat. But it must work all the time, for boats of this design, with a cutaway keel or a fin, have to be steered almost all the time. They will not readily hold a course, particularly with the wind and sea behind them.

*Cu Na Mara* didn't actually have a keel. She had a bronze centerboard which is a bronze fin let down from the bottom of the hull. This fin fitted into a housing below her hull which was shaped to produce the effect of a shallow keel. When her centerboard was up, *Cu Na Mara* drew only three feet. With her centerboard down, she drew close to nine feet.

This reduction of the length and area of the keel and development of the spade rudder are modern trends in yacht design resulting from racing experience. They derive from the need to tack quickly and from the belief that the less boat there is in the water, the faster the boat will go. But there are drawbacks. As already explained, the rudder now takes over much of the work previously handled by the keel. It has to be put far aft where it is completely unsupported. Often it still has to be made so big that the man at the wheel is worn out after an hour or so of work. So the rudder is then balanced—that is, an area has to be added ahead of the rudderpost and below the waterline to help the helmsman turn the rudder. This area, while helping the helmsman, detracts from the efficiency of the rudder and puts a greater strain on it.

Well, *Cu Na Mara* had a spade rudder and I was going to race her to Hawaii, so I would very soon have some practical experience of spade rudders.

I had no time at all in which to tune *Cu Na Mara* for her unofficial race to Hawaii. Her sails were lost by the airline transporting them to the United States and days of frustration were spent locating them. They had been taken off the plane in Chicago and put on another to Denver, and in fact given a grand tour of the continental United States before they reached Los Angeles.

When they got here, the whole staff of the air parcel company to which they were consigned quit work—not over my sails, it's true, but that did not make them easier to find. And when they were found, the spinnaker was missing. A telephone call to England disclosed that through a misunderstanding no spinnaker had been made. But Mr. Handfield, of Cranfield and Carter, said he would make me one in three days. He was as good as his word and that sail arrived just four days before the start of the Transpac and was a beautiful fit. Which shows that when the English want to hurry, they can give lessons to us all.

Anyway there was no time for tuning the rigging and the angle of *Cu Na Mara*'s mast was a matter of guesswork. The tension of her lower shrouds, which would come into use under heavy strain, was also a matter of guesswork.

My crew were mostly teenagers, headed by my son Kevin who had, at fourteen, already made one voyage to Hawaii with me. With him was my second eldest son, Christopher, fourteen, and Mark Kerwin, a friend of theirs, who was sixteen, and a young Canadian from New Brunswick, Rick Flewellyn, who at twenty was the oldest of the crew. All had sailing experience and Rick, a tall, blond, cheerful young man, had sailed a fifty-foot yawl, *Kwan Yin,* to Los Angeles from Boston. She had lost her masts in a blow in the Bay of Tehuantepec, but Rick had stuck with her and proved a fine seaman in every way. So the crew was sound and tried. As far as boat and sails were concerned all were new and untried. Equipped with but three sails—Genoa, main and a light weather spinnaker, *Cu Na Mara* was hardly fit for ocean racing. And I had had half a day only in which to try out the spinnaker, and that in a wind so light the sail would not fill.

Stores had been put aboard in the days while I hunted my sails about the country. Also put aboard were all the gear demanded by the Transpac Committee. We had two man-overboard-poles and six life jackets, each with its own waterproof flashlight, Coast Guard approved. We had two horseshoe life rings, an inflatable rubber raft and a dinghy. We had flares to hold in our hands and flares to fire into the air and we had sea dye and that expensive shark repellent which sharks find so delicious. *Cu Na Mara*'s water tanks were pressed full and I had fifteen gallons additional in plastic jugs of a gallon each. Her gasoline tanks were full, also, for the engine (in neutral) would be run an hour each day to keep her batteries charged. Sails excepted, we had on board everything possessed by the official contenders of whom there were seventy-two.

The start of the race was to be off the Point Fermin buoy, outside San Pedro, July 4th. We took *Cu Na Mara* down to San Pedro the day before the race and put her in a slip at the San Pedro Boat Works. She was new to me and new to my crew and new to the ocean. She was so new, in fact, that I was not yet familiar with her storage space. She was so new, in fact, that nobody but Rick knew how to light the alcohol stove on which all our cooking was to be done—he having handled that make of stove before. When we had docked the boat, I asked someone to light the stove and make me a cup of tea while I went ashore to make a phone call.

When I got back to the slip, the boat was on fire. Her whole cabin was a mess of flames. I leaped aboard and a second later Kevin, covered in white powder, put his head out of the cabin hatch and said he had got the fire out. He had an extinguisher in his hand.

It was the alcohol stove which had nearly destroyed the boat. Alcohol, under pressure, had squirted out of the tank and caught fire and the flames had mounted to the cabin roof. Kevin had had the presence of mind to grab a fire extinguisher and go to work with it. The whole interior of the boat was now covered with fine white powder, but the boat was saved and so was my son.

We set to work to clear up the mess and I began to wonder—between the sails not arriving, the boat being a couple of feet too short to compete officially, and the alcohol stove catching fire the first time it was used—whether *Cu Na Mara* might not be a bad luck ship.

That stove caught fire so many times afterwards that we got used to it. I don't know how insurance companies allow such equipment on board a boat. It had this saving grace: since the fuel it used was alcohol, the fire could be put out by dumping a bucket of water all over the stove. But often on the voyage that followed I would say to Kevin, "Set fire to the stove and make me a cup of tea, please."

And set fire to the stove is what he did, as often as not.

# *Chapter Three*

WE DIDN'T SEE the start of the Transpac that year—which was something of a surprise. The starting area had been cleared of all boats and the area cleared was so vast that there were times that morning when I thought perhaps it extended into international waters. We met picket boat after picket boat which directed us seaward and still seaward until the starting yachts were but scraps of white fluttering on the distant horizon. That, however, was still not far enough. When we got to the last picket boat not a glimpse of the starting fleet was to be seen. And then we were told that that last picket boat represented the end of the starting line—a starting line a mile long?—and we must keep seaward even of it.

My plan had been to wait for the starting gun and cross the line outside at the uncluttered end so as not to interfere with anybody. There was not now, so far seaward had we been ushered, a yacht within half a mile of us. I heard the five-minute gun (on the radiotelephone) and sailed away from the extension of the starting line for two minutes, then rounded up, and headed for the utterly empty "line," which was at least half a mile from the seaward end of the starting line itself. I was about to cross it as I heard the starting gun go off (on the radiotelephone, we could not hear it directly) when a powerboat roared down on me and the man at the wheel shouted: "Where the hell do you think you are going? You can't cross that line." Deputised by the United States Coast Guard, he had had a rush of power to the head. I fell off and stood out to sea sadly and then, trimming sail, headed for Honolulu, two thousand miles away. The Coast Guard auxiliary in the powerboat, his duty done, headed back for San Pedro, four miles off. I hope he made it.

The rules of the Transpac demand that the island of Catalina be left to port and this meant that the wind, which was southwesterly, would soon head us.

There is only one reliable rule concerning weather and I learned it from a doctor who applied it in medicine. It is this: "Normal conditions normally prevail." So if you have spots here and there around your waistline and your eyes hurt when you look into a bright light, you are more likely to be suffering from measles than Rocky Mountain Spotted Fever. And if the wind is southwesterly in Southern California, it will veer to the west and then die off to nothing for an hour or so. Then, with luck, it will come in strong again from the west and perhaps veer further to the northwest, for a westerly or northwesterly is the normal wind in Southern California.

I knew then, at the start of the race, that we were going to have nothing but zephyrs for some time. This would favor *Cu Na Mara* for small boats can go faster than large boats in light airs. We must make the best of the southwesterly and try to clear the west end of Catalina before it died away altogether. The west end of Catalina is a trap for yachts, providing a big lee. I recall one Transpacer—*Staghound* I believe she was—who lay two days off the west end of Catalina, caught in the lee, while the rest of the fleet who had got clear, creamed away for Honolulu.

An hour after the start we were able to see the rest of the fleet over against the coast of the mainland. They were about four miles downwind of us and *Stormvogel* (readily distinguishable by her split rig and her size) was perhaps a quarter of a mile ahead. It seemed there was a trifle more wind over there than where we were, and the classic Transpac tactic on this first leg is to make short tacks up the California coast, until Catalina can be cleared for there is a favoring current inshore.

The Transpac, once started, divides itself into three distinct problems on the accurate solution of which success depends.

The first problem is to get past the west end of Catalina, usually in light and dying winds. The race always starts at noon; the end of the island is about twenty-two miles from the starting line and it must be passed before sunset for there is a high probability of the wind dying with the sun. An hour or five hours may be lost turning circles off Catalina if that point is not cleared by dark. But what, you ask, do four or five hours matter in a race which is going to last fourteen or sixteen days? They have this significance. If your competitor hits the trade winds four or five hours ahead of you, he will gain ten or maybe fifteen miles on you, and if you should have only light winds while he has twenty knots of wind, the distance will be greater in his favor. The fascination of ocean racing is that, just like inshore racing, every minute counts. The difference is that every minute counts over a much longer time.

Once Catalina is cleared, the next problem is to get to the trade winds at the earliest possible moment. The trade winds sweep in a huge arc from south to north off the California coast. South, off Mexico and Central America, they are much closer to the shore than off California where the cold westerlies deflect them seaward. The problem is whether to head directly for the Hawaiian Islands on a course of roughly west southwest when you can expect to find the trades on the fourth or fifth day out, or whether to head more to the south, sailing an additional hundred miles perhaps, but picking up the trades a day or maybe a day and a half earlier.

Vital to the decision is a weather system called the North Pacific High. This is an area of some hundreds of miles in extent (though the size and the shape of the area vary from day to day), in which winds are mere zephyrs ranging from zero to five miles an hour. This high usually lies on the direct route from San Pedro to Honolulu. So most skippers decide not to sail the straight line but to sail an S-shape across the ocean. They drop more to the south to find the trades. Once they have the trades, they start heading back to the rhumb line—the direct line to the islands—and perhaps go a trifle north of it. Then as they close in on the islands (always avoiding the High) they start going south again making a very drawn-out S-curve across the eastern reaches of the Pacific.

On the Transpac of 1967, the problem of whether to go south or north was academic. The major difficulty was to find any kind of wind with which to sail in any direction. The wind fell lighter and lighter, veering as expected into the west. Then it died away completely and we slatted around in a confused chop. The sun sank and Catalina was still ahead of us. Gradually the sea died until it became as smooth as silk. I set the watches and went below, thankful that in this calm sea I would not be plagued by the waves of seasickness which overcome me inevitably during my first two days at sea. About three in the morning Kevin, who had the wheel, called me.

"Dad," he said, "I can hear seals barking."

A muddy picture of a famous Thurber cartoon came to my mind . . . the wife waking her husband up in the small hours and saying, "I think I hear a seal barking," and there, on the headboard of the bed, is a seal.

"So what?" I said and rolled over. And then the significance of seals sank into my consciousness. Seals meant rocks, possibly land! I flung out of my bunk, into the cockpit, and listened. And sure enough from somewhere astern came the sharp angry barks of seals. There was no wind at all. Around us lay a silver fog and peering over the side I found strands of kelp floating in the water. Kelp meant rocks and seals meant rocks and the problem was: were we drifting down on those rocks or were we drifting away from them. And what rocks were they?

We had managed to weather the west end of Catalina at ten the previous evening while I was asleep. We had since then not been able to sail any allotted course. Only catpaws of wind had offered, for three minutes, five minutes, twelve minutes. These had been followed by calms during which we drifted wherever tide or current took us. The course we had tried to follow was west, and west would take us past Catalina to Point Dume thrusting out from the California coast into the Pacific. There were rocks off Point Dume. There were seals off Point Dume. And there was kelp off Point Dume. Despite the uncertainty about our position resulting from the combination of light airs, fog and night, having suggested itself, the thought that we were close to Point Dume persisted until it became not speculation but conviction. Had I then had to send out a call for help, I would have given our position as one mile west of Point Dume. In which case, everybody would have drowned.

I took the wheel and, nudging the boat along a westward course, peered around in the mist for a glimpse of the light which I believed would glow on a buoy off Point Dume. At last I saw it on the starboard bow winking away, yellow and reassuring.

Our course would lead us clear of it and making only a fraction of a knot, I held on, using every little breath of air I could find. Then below the light I had seen appeared another—a green light. A green light at Point Dume? Well —there might be. No light list for the California coast had been issued for several years at this time. My charts were four years out of date. It was not impossible that a green light had been put on the Point Dume buoy and that the yellow light had been moved ashore. In any case I was clear of both lights and crawled on to pass them to starboard. Then it seemed that the tide started to flood and moved *Cu Na Mara* eastward so that she could no longer clear those two lights.

Should I tack, which would mean calling up the crew? Or should I hold on? I decided to hold on. We were making not miles per hour, but yards per hour through the water. Even if that were a rocky coast dead ahead we had plenty of time in which to go about in this flat sea.

But those lights were very puzzling, particularly when a third light appeared a little aft of the first yellow light and a little lower. And then below these lights I began to detect, as the dawn approached and the mist thinned, the structures on which they were mounted. They were tall thin structures, dark in the pewter of the mist. Finally I saw that I was not approaching a transformed Point Dume at all, but a remarkably big ketch, whose masthead light I had mistaken for the light on the Point Dume buoy. She had several hands on deck and she was busy hauling up and taking down the greater part of her light weather sail wardrobe. I saw a light drifter go up and a light spinnaker and a light mizzen staysail. A whisper of wind, encouraged by the dawn, had sprung up, and we went by making perhaps a knot.

"Who are you?" cried the ketch.

"*Cu Na Mara*. And you?"

"*Chiriqui*."

"Are you sure you are not the Point Dume light?" I inquired. But when I consulted the chart, I found that there is no Point Dume light. (A good precept for those who are lost in fog is this: the buoy you pass or the light you see or the foghorn you hear very probably isn't the one you want it to be.)

The sighting of *Chiriqui* left unanswered the mystery of the kelp and the seals. I still did not know where we were and neither, I think, did *Chiriqui* though we refrained from asking each other. Although I was not racing, it is one of the rules of ocean races that no information about position may be obtained from another vessel.

My best guess (Point Dume being wrong) was that we were somewhere in mid-channel between Santa Catalina Island and tiny Santa Barbara Island. The seals? Well, sometimes in calm water seals venture out into mid-channel and, fishing at night, amuse themselves by barking. Kelp? It was just drifting around and did not signify that land was close at hand.

That is all guessing. I have since then been over the charts most carefully and done my best to place my position. But all that effort is really no better than my guess—mid-channel between Catalina and Santa Barbara.

The day that followed, the second of the race, was once more a painful matter of drifting and sailing by catpaws. By evening we had worked our way to Santa Barbara Island, having covered in eighteen hours perhaps forty miles.

It was obvious that no records were going to be set in the Transpac that year, and we spent the time coaxing all we could out of the boat and getting everything shipshape. One task I was grateful for the chance to do was that of affixing the waterproof flashlights to all the lifejackets and seeing that they worked. Then Mark, who loves fishing, got out a line. He caught a blue shark. It was not a big shark—about four feet long at the most. Mark reeled it alongside, and it looked at us through its coffin eyes. He pulled its wicked head a little out of the water and Rick made a grab for the tail. He got the tail, and the shark whipped around and made a snap at his hand that missed by centimeters. The effort broke the line and off the shark went. Then came darkness and once more the night watches and uncertainty in dark and fog.

All day the most wind we had had was six knots. As the sun set the wind died again. We turned circle after circle in the water with Santa Barbara Island close by now. The seals we heard this time we knew were on the island. The kelp which caught on our spade rudder, rendering the boat quite unmanageable until dislodged, was also from Santa Barbara Island. So went the long night, amid seals and calm and kelp. At dawn came a very light wind out of the south. We caught up with a large yawl or ketch, some distance off, for the very light wind favored our small size. A little later we came upon a large sloop, but again could not identify her. All the time there were but catpaws of wind.

However, around ten, the wind came in steady from the southwest. We could see over to port the long shape of San Nicolas Island and all around us, in every quadrant of the horizon, were yachts. We were in the middle of the Transpac fleet. Some were close inshore by San Nicolas, working the current that sweeps around the island just outside the kelp. Others were north of us and still others ahead of us. I counted thirteen. Broad on our starboard beam was a Cal 36 and as the wind stiffened we kept pace with her for mile after mile. Then the wind performed a kind of miracle.

Within half an hour of its arrival, it swept the ocean clear of boats except for the Cal 36 to leeward of us. Even with the glasses I could see only one or two sails far to the south.

Everybody, then, was heading southward, looking for the trades. The Cal 36 and *Cu Na Mara* alone headed west toward the sunset. By dawn the Cal 36 had gone and we were alone on the ocean.

# *Chapter Four*

AT THE START of a long-distance ocean race there is a period of intense activity and concentration when everybody is on deck and everybody is working to sail the boat at its best because all the competitors are in sight. It seems essential to hold even with or to pass a sloop ahead or to leeward, or not to be overtaken by a yawl or ketch astern. But such a pace cannot be maintained.

As phase two of the race sets in, a routine is established of watches on and off. The business of ship-keeping becomes intermingled with the business of ship sailing. The meals have to be cooked three times a day. The dishes have to be washed. Bunks have to be kept straightened and sails have to be stowed in such a way that they can be got at day or night, fair weather or foul, without great difficulty. And five or six men who probably could not stand each other's company daily at an office or a club for two weeks are required to so adjust that they can stand not merely each other's company but the very closest association with each other, day and night, in an area which, in *Cu Na Mara*'s case, was at its extreme thirty-four feet long and ten feet wide.

On a sailing yacht the men must learn to occupy each other's beds and to respect each other's repose. The noisy fellow who cannot come below with less sound than the Bulgarian cavalry about to debauch a nunnery must learn to amend his habit of noise and move about his business in quiet if not in prayer. The fussy fellow who, once in his bunk, decides to get up and look for a cookie, and then for a pair of glasses, and then for a sock which he saw lying on the cabin sole during the day, must learn to leave such matters be so his crewmates can get their proper sleep.

Little habits of selfishness or unconcern for others will, in such cramped quarters, induce enormous quantities of rage in others which they must learn to control. Yet I confess that I was never so angered with one man as with a shipmate who, after washing his teeth, left the wash basin smeared with toothpaste day after day after day until I exploded. He, however, was not even conscious of the fact that he did not rinse the washbasin after washing his teeth. His mother, it seems, had always done it for him.

The position of the skipper on an ocean race is one of extreme delicacy. He must establish and maintain authority. He must keep everybody aware of the fact that the tenth day at sea is just as important as the first or the last as far as the race is concerned. He must never take sides in the little quarrels that break out between members of his crew, because when they are ready to make up it is he who will be the link between them, and if he has shown sympathy, one way or another, he will have damaged that delicate and important position of peacemaker.

I do not myself belong to the buddy-buddy class of skippers. I find that if you do not establish a position of authority and respect then someone else on board will, for that is human nature. You can't really lay down rules for being a good skipper (and I am not at all sure that I qualify anyway) because beyond command there is also involved the matter of fairness and humor and patience.

One thing is important. If, as skipper, you should lose patience and bawl out a man unfairly before his mates, then you must apologise to him before the rest of his fellows. It is much better not to bawl out anybody unless milder approaches have failed to rectify a repeated error. Personally, I never shout at my crew during the first week at sea. Thereafter, I shout at them quite often—sometimes justly and sometimes out of sheer weariness and then, of course, an apology is called for and I make it.

As for the crewman who finds himself always at odds with his skipper, I recommend to him the many single-handed long-distance races which are now available across the Atlantic and across the Pacific. On these he can be captain and crew in one, and second guess himself all the way across the ocean.

It is not easy to be skipper, for very many judgments and decisions have to be made and in the nature of things most of these are likely to be wrong. The skipper must judge the set of the sails and what sails should be carried, the weather now and the weather to come, the weather at dusk and what it is likely to be at midnight, and the skill of each individual man at the wheel and his competence in handling the ship should the wind or sea build up in the small hours, the physical shape his crew is in individually and collectively, the physical condition of his ship (which will not be the same at the end of the race as it was at the beginning), whether the food is ample and sufficiently appetizing, whether someone is shirking in some small duty, like washing dishes, and causing resentment, whether to fall off half a point, ease the ship and sail another hundred miles, or whether to hold on with the ship jolting about and sail a hundred miles less. And so on and on.

There is nothing that does not come within the skipper's realm and few things among these he can afford to neglect. On some boats the skipper does not stand a regular watch, but comes on deck at odd intervals, day and night, when he feels it necessary. On a boat the size of *Cu Na Mara* this would leave the crew standing too many hours of night watch, so I elected to stand my watch at the wheel although I was also navigating. I was, however, relieved of cooking.

It is in the second day at sea that you can separate the racing sailors from the cruising sailors on an ocean race. Most crews become cruising sailors on the second or third day. Winning crews remain racing men. The difference is slight but all important. The cruising man, once a sail is drawing well, leaves it so for hour after hour after hour. He doesn't care if by a little adjustment here or there he can pick up an extra fraction of a mile an hour. The racing sailor, however, is conscious all the while of the need to keep the boat footing along at its best possible speed—whether it is blowing like thunder or not enough wind stirs to put out a match.

The best way to retain that highly competitive attitude is to imagine another yacht sailing alongside you. Then you will find yourself trimming sail as needed, watching your course, keeping an eye on the seas, and keeping a watch on your speed. But when all there is about you is the void of the ocean, rolling on without limit and without any imaginable limit (after four days at sea it is often hard to realize that there will ever be land on the horizon—or ever was), then it is very difficult to keep up the racing spirit. But it must be done. Long-distance races are, according to the winners, won in every mile that is sailed—not just in the last few miles to the finish line.

On the third day out then we met the ocean wind and the ocean, and settled down to the game in earnest.

# *Chapter Five*

THE WIND HAD come up on the third day, very light and from the south. It went around to the southwest and should have then died, for some time at least, for that is the rule in Southern California. However, perhaps because we were now a hundred miles offshore, this petering southwesterly continued to veer until it was a true westerly and then a northwesterly and then, gaining confidence and zest, it piped up to twenty knots to the delight of all.

Actually, we had moved into the wind belt out of the coastal weather and with the northwesterly to speed us along I decided to go south, joining in the race to the trades, although the mighty *Stormvogel,* according to the radio, had kept on the northern route and was making all westing possible before turning south for the islands.

This northwest wind did not set in firmly until dusk of the third day, when watches were set for the night—two hours on and eight hours off, for we had luxury in watch-keeping aboard *Cu Na Mara.* These short watches at the wheel meant only one man on deck at a time. He had a lifeline about him securing him to the ship and on a lanyard around his neck he had a whistle on which he had but to blow a sharp blast to summon all hands. This system worked excellently and gave me a rested crew all the way to Hawaii.

During that first night of real ocean wind, it became plain that there was something wrong with *Cu Na Mara.* The course set was 210 magnetic, which was around 194 by the true compass as the magnetic card is pulled about 16 degrees eastward of true north in Southern California. When it was time for my watch I found, on examining the log, that nobody had been able to steer closer to the true course than 240 degrees by compass. The wind had gone around to north northwest and was still blowing a good twenty knots. But no matter how hard her helm was put over, *Cu Na Mara* sailed up into the wind, her sails overpowering her rudder.

I took over from Rick at four that morning and found that with the wheel hard over, and in fact lashed in that position, *Cu Na Mara* could only just be kept from flying right up into the wind like a weathercock. To correct this, thinking that the mainsail was overpowering the spade rudder (which I had not liked in the first place), we reefed the main. This had no noticeable effect. Then I slacked off the main completely and trimmed the Genoa in tight. There was still no difference. We experimented with the centerboard. We dropped it all the way down, raised it all the way up, and left it halfway up. In not one of these positions was there the slightest change in the steering. *Cu Na Mara* still fought her helm and tried her best to get up into the wind.

The evidence indicated that the spade rudder was inadequate. But Charles Morgan is a well known designer and it was impossible that he should have designed a boat which could not be kept out of the wind in a twenty-knot blow. At the end of my watch, while breakfast was being made, I considered the problem carefully and remembered that something of the sort had once happened aboard *Bahia.* While heading up the Molokai Channel, she had refused to answer her helm and fall off the wind. The reason was that she had no helm to answer. Some work had been done on her in a shipyard in Hawaii and the connective mechanism between her wheel and her rudder had been left slack.

I took the wheel from Kevin, who had relieved me, and greatly daring, put it up to windward, which, if the rudder was working, would have flung us up into the wind and perhaps put us over on the other tack. Nothing happened. We had no rudder. *Cu Na Mara* was sailing strictly on her sail trim.

"Rick," I said, "after breakfast (for Rick was eating with his usual dash) get some handtools and check the steering quadrant. Either we have lost the rudder blade or the quadrant is loose." Happily the trouble lay with the quadrant. A key had come loose in the clamp which fastened the quadrant to the rudderpost. When the wheel was moved there was only a small and uncertain amount of movement in the rudder itself. Rick found the key—he was both a top hand and a good mechanic—and put it back in place. The repair lasted five hours. At that point, Rick, who has an appalling love of pulling things entirely to pieces to find out what ails them, again took the tools and remained a suspiciously long time grunting in the cramped space below the cockpit floor.

"What is taking you so long?" I asked eventually.

"Well," said Rick, poking his curly head up into the fresh

air, "the only way to fix this thing is to take the whole kit and caboodle to pieces . . ."

"Out of there, you rogue," I shouted. "You're not going to tear my rudder to pieces in mid-ocean." Out came Rick and I replaced him in the cramped, coffin-shaped area under the cockpit floor. In his enthusiasm for a thorough repair, Rick had already undone one of the steering cables and started in on the other. I refastened them and tightened up the clamp that held the key in place. Smaller than Rick, I was able to get a better grip on the wrench. Then we got under way again, having lost three hours—perhaps fifteen miles—during the course of the repair. But this time the repair lasted to the end of the voyage, though in the heavy going later we were all of us troubled, during our watches, as to how long the rudder would last. There was no mistake in design or poor engineering here; the incident merely served to emphasize what it is easy to overlook or forget—the one part of a boat that works all the time on any voyage is the rudder. And spade rudders work harder than any other.

That morning, with San Nicolas Island lost over the horizon and a day's sail away, I took the first sights of the voyage, and found that in three days of sailing we had made only two hundred and twenty miles. That was very poor going, the result of the light winds at the start of the race. I waited for the noon sun to get my latitude and then looked about for the ocean pilot chart on which to plot the ship's position. It was then that I found that there were no ocean charts on board. I was quite sure that I had brought two of them onto the ship. I was quite sure that I had stowed them under the mattress on my bunk. But they were neither there nor anywhere else.

You may be sure that at that moment I had a surge of

panic. What, I asked myself, was the latitude and longitude of the Hawaiian Islands? Twenty something north and one fifty-five or so west? But how horrible to be headed only in general terms toward my goal. My panic subsided when I remembered that I had several charts of the islands themselves aboard. From these I took the coordinates needed and on the back of a plotting chart drew my own pilot chart for the voyage. This I stuck up on a bulkhead in the main cabin and all were relieved to see it, for it is a great comfort to know the latitude and longitude of the place toward which you are going, where you are at any particular time, and the course to be steered to your destination.

Each day at noon I marked off the position of the ship on the chart. And each day at noon I endured the silent reproaches of my crew when they felt that we had not gone far enough considering the weight of the wind and the splendid sailing each had experienced during his watch or alternatively I drew looks of disbelief when my navigation showed runs of great length and I had, in justification, to mutter about favorable currents, the constancy of the wind and so forth.

Alas, the navigator is always suspect. It is somehow his fault if the day's run is not up to expectation. And it is he who is suspect if the day's run is so long as to be difficult to believe. He has but one fleeting moment of triumph—when land is sighted. And it had better be the land he predicted and not some other land. But the navigator has his consolation, too. Despite the suspicion with which he is regarded, he has a kind of power over the boat in the eyes of the crew, saying where it will be and what course it is best to steer (the final decision as to course is in the hands of the skipper). Also he has communion and brotherhood of a kind with the sun and the moon and the stars. The mighty sun whispers to him where the ship now lies and the moon silent and remote points his way across the ocean. And the stars! Ah, God's lovely stars—how faithful they are in their position and in their shining. What consolation there is in them in all the disorders of the world and what a sense of continuity they give to our brief lives. For that same star that guided Ulysses guided also *Cu Na Mara.* How terrible the world would be without these little lights of hope.

We were then bowling southward—south to the trades blowing strong over the rejoicing ocean. With the steering restored, the pilot chart made, and the wind mightily in the northwest, I headed *Cu Na Mara* on the course I believed would bring her most quickly to the trade wind belt. The wind was a point aft of her beam. Satisfied that this was so I proposed to all hands that we raise the spinnaker to speed our arrival in the belt of the trade winds.

Kevin and Rick immediately went forward to handle the sail and its rigging while Mark and Christopher remained in the cockpit to man sheets and guy lines. I took the wheel believing that I could by reasoning do whatever was needed with the boat at the critical moment when the spinnaker, like some mighty genie, rose out of its bag.

You must realize this was only the third time that we had raised the spinnaker on *Cu Na Mara.* It was the third time that I had been at the wheel when the spinnaker was raised. It was blowing twenty miles an hour and the seas were vigorous and cresting. The sail was got out on the foredeck in silence and the interminable business of attaching all the rigging that makes a spinnaker so complicated was begun.

I will list here for you the lines which are attached to a spinnaker and if you are familiar with them forgive me, for there are many who are not experienced in this area.

First there is the spinnaker net, which on *Cu Na Mara*

is raised on the jib halyard. It is precisely what the name implies, a net in the shape of a jib sail, drawn tight in the fore triangle of the vessel. Its purpose is to prevent the spinnaker from embracing the forestay—which it will do with purpose and grace whenever the opportunity presents itself. Then there is the spinnaker halyard which goes to its own block at the masthead. It is better to have this block rigged so that it can stand out from the mast on a pendant and move from side to side, but it must also clear the top of the jib stay or there will be much gnashing of teeth should it tangle with the head of that stay. (Remember the first law of ropes, lines, pendants, anchor rodes, etcetera: that which is free to move will invariably entangle itself in some place where you cannot get at it.) After the spinnaker net and halyard there is the topping lift which raises the spinnaker pole so that the weight of the pole does not rest on the sail. In very light winds, this weight would dump the air out of the spinnaker. Then there is the downhaul which prevents the spinnaker pole from rising and giving the mast a good clout with its outboard end. Then there is the guy which holds the spinnaker pole in position. One guy goes aft and another is sometimes (though not always) rigged forward. The aft guy is best rigged to one corner of the spinnaker and then passed through a fitting at the end of the spinnaker pole. This method has the advantage that you can let the guy go and it will stream through the fitting and collapse the sail which can then be pulled in by the sheet—and there is often a critical need for collapsing the sail in dealing with spinnakers. The disadvantage to this method of rigging is that the guy tends to chafe where it passes through the fitting at the end of the spinnaker pole. Finally, there is the sheet on the spinnaker. Aft guy and sheet are led to the farthest possible point aft and on the way they usually manage to get on the wrong side of shrouds and lifelines unless rigged by experts. They are then led around winches for they must be trimmed mechanically. From there they are belayed to cleats.

When all this rigging is in place, and the leads of the various lines have been thoroughly checked, the spinnaker may be raised. Up to this point it is contained in its bag; the head attached to the halyard and the two lower corners (clews) one to the sheet and the other to the guy leading through the spinnaker pole. The pole is always to windward. The time has now come for the foredeck crew to say a short prayer that all will be well and the spinnaker will go up without twisting or "hour glassing," that is, getting a twist in the middle so that the top and bottom fill with air while the middle is horridly turned around upon itself.

Kevin and Rick, having got all these details of rigging straightened out and having ensured that the spinnaker bag was tied to the deck so that it would not go overboard when emptied of the sail, said they were ready. Mark and Christopher, in the cockpit, assured me that they were ready to trim guy and sheet. The pole had been positioned at about right angles to the wind direction. I swallowed hard, put the helm downwind, and shouted, "Break her out, then!"

It went up beautifully. It streamed snow white and gold and soft out of its little bag and it enveloped the heavens. It filled with all the fullness of the breast of a pouter pigeon and *Cu Na Mara,* taken for a moment in breathless surprise, heeled in the water and then started to seethe southward with a zest to inspire poetry.

What beautiful, silent, soaring power. What magnificence. What lithe grace and beauty and perfection. Certainly, I told myself, I had been a fool to take so old-fashioned and crabbed a view of such a lovely sail. And even as I berated myself for stuffy narrowness of view, the block by which the spinnaker was held aloft on its halyard exploded and the whole damn thing floated mockingly down, glided into the water and diving, sought to entangle itself around the rudder. We gathered it in in silence, like at the burial of Sir John Moore, and put the whole sopping, bedraggled mess down in the cabin, where it wet everything in sight including the toilet paper in the head. And then I asked in a quiet, restrained, and patient voice what had happened and Rick said in a quiet, restrained, and patient voice that the stinking, foreign-made, no good, plastic, lousy halyard block had pulled the swivel out of its evil and pointed head and come down on the deck. And to prove this he showed me the block. The sight was impressive. Not only had the swivel pulled clean out, but the braided line which formed the spinnaker halyard had imprinted the pattern of its grain on the plastic pulley of the block. That could only have been done under great strain. Having seen this evidence of the vast tonnage of the wind in a full spinnaker, I took a look at the backstay and the turnbuckle by which the spinnaker was set up and the chainplate by which it was fastened to the transom of the boat. For all that strain was transmitted to these items. They seemed unharried.

You will have missed an important part of my earlier homily on the position of a skipper on a racing yacht if you failed to realise that it was now my duty to go to the top of the mast and replace the broken spinnaker halyard block with a new one. One day I may be able to make an ocean voyage under sail without having to go to the masthead, but that will be when I go as cook—an unlikely development. We got out the bosun's chair and I took a look about at the sea and felt the wind and realized that it was going to be a little rough aloft. I lashed a bucket to the chair and put in it a pair of pliers, some soft galvanized wire, a couple of blocks, a piece of line, and a screwdriver. We hooked the chair to the jib halyard and up I went. It was a tedious, nervewracking, miserable task, hard on the crew who were winching me up and hard on me for I had to grab with hands and feet to prevent being smashed against the mast or sent flying into the stainless-steel rigging by the rough sea and wind. Chris took the wheel and put the boat downwind to ease the motion aloft which of course is enormously exaggerated from that on deck. At the masthead, though I locked myself to the mast with my feet, leaving my hands free to work, I was jerked about miserably which made the very simple task of replacing the spinnaker halyard block quite difficult.

I became tired just from the effort needed to prevent myself being swung around the masthead or bashed into it. However, I am sure that much of my ordeal was the result of pure nerves and after a little while I found that I could relax a little. This helped and after I got the block rigged I took a look about the ocean. The shape of the boat below me was a lovely wedge, slim and toylike. Christopher was a small, anxious doll in the cockpit and the seas were frosted with silver from horizon to horizon. Away to the east was a purple mountain range of clouds and southward the waves fled in liquid lines streaked with foam. The length of these waves, seen from on high, was impressive. How long were they—a quarter of a mile, half a mile? There was nothing in the empty sea and sky against which to measure their size. On and on they rolled, now and again rearing up like stallions, galloping, tossing high their heads and manes. On and on, in fury and in joy, the freest things on earth with thousands of miles in which to sport.

I returned to the deck with reluctance for the deck belonged to a petty world and up there I had caught a glimpse of something far more magnificent.

# *Chapter Six*

It is very hard without instruments to judge the speed of the wind. How fast you think it is blowing often depends upon how nervous you feel and how much confidence you have in your boat. A fifteen-mile-an-hour wind is only a moderate breeze in a sailboat of any size, but it is half a gale in a rowboat, and a wind of forty knots which has been weathered many a time by yachts of moderate size has been known to set up a blow that buckled the plates of ocean liners.

Admiral Sir Francis Beaufort of revered memory, way back in 1806 devised a scale against which the force (not the speed) of the wind could be measured. His scale of twelve gradations went from zero—a flat calm—to Force 12—a wind "that no canvas could withstand." The Beaufort scale correlates wind force to wave size and appearance. It is beloved by the British, particularly yachtsmen, who describe sailing in Force Six or Force Seven conditions.

In America, yachtsmen like to give wind speed, not wind

force. So they talk of a twenty-knot blow, which is the Englishman's Force 6 and was called by Admiral Beaufort a "strong breeze." The two methods of estimating the impact of the wind have now been put together and speeds in miles per hour assigned to the numbered Forces of Admiral Beaufort. Gales, according to the wind scale now recognized by both the United States and Britain, start at thirty-two miles an hour and a whole gale, Force 10, starts at fifty-five miles an hour. A hurricane, which Admiral Beaufort sagely remarked no canvas could withstand, starts with winds of over seventy-five miles an hour.

Most racing yachts now have wind gauges at their mastheads but I had no such refinement aboard *Cu Na Mara* and measured the wind like old Beaufort did. I took a look at the height and shape of the waves and the amount of cresting they were doing and announced the wind speed to anyone who cared to believe me.

After two days of calms we were getting plenty of wind. By midday of July 8th, four days after the start of the race, we had an eighteen-mile-an-hour wind out of the north (by my reckoning) and we were about four hundred miles from San Pedro. That was slow going, but it was more cheering to realize that three hundred of those miles had been done in two days, so we were averaging a hundred and fifty miles a day now that we had the wind. We still had not had the spinnaker aloft for any length of time.

I was having trouble getting a morning or afternoon sight for longitude. The skies were overcast, the sea rough, and if the truth must be told, I was feeling a little seasick. It is depressing how nauseated you can get looking through the small telescope of a sextant at a heaving horizon over which the ball of the sun lurches and swoops as you try to bring it in contact with the uncertain edge of the world. Of my latitude, I had no doubt. I had managed to get a good meridian shot at noon on July 8th and over and above that I had sighted a bosun bird. The meridian shot said that my latitude was 31.10 north and this was confirmed by the bosun bird, with his long white tail and fluttering wings, for these little creatures will scarcely venture north of the 31st parallel.

The bosun bird gave notice that we were approaching the trade wind belt. That evening a school of porpoises snorted and rollicked about the ship. That night the deck log spoke of fluky winds wavering from northwest to north—another sign of the approach of the trades. The seas now began to moderate and the wind to be less boisterous, though still steady. We were averaging seven knots on a direct course for the islands. Things were going so well indeed that I proposed once again to set the spinnaker. This time we broke one of the carriages on which the inboard end of the pole rides on the mast. It broke because the downhaul was not rigged and the pole rode up in the air and broke the ring on the carriage.

However, we kept the spinnaker up for two hours and then took it down for *Cu Na Mara* just didn't like that sail. She tried to ride up to windward and it took quick work at the wheel to stop her. An hour of that was enough for a helmsman and we found our shoulder muscles aching from the exercise.

The wheel had to be put hard over, away from the wind, to prevent *Cu Na Mara* from broaching—that is, coming around broadside to the wind when, with her spinnaker flying, she would undoubtedly be knocked down in the water. Sailing with the spinnaker was nervous and exacting work for the helmsman; rather like trying to run downstairs with a plate full of Jello when the penalty for dropping any on the floor is that the whole house blows up.

That day, the eighth of July, we had a further sign of our approach to the trade wind area. A tiny squid flipped out of the water onto the deck, falling almost at the feet of Motley, a little kitten with a multi-colored coat whom we had brought as ship's cat. Motley sniffed this gift and then started to growl. She gave a low, cautious growl like a somewhat savage purr, and then demolished that tiny squid in a trice. All that was left of it were two bones as fine as needles. Discovering that such gifts might now and again be expected, Motley from that moment forward took a tremendous interest in the ocean. She would sit watching the water as intently as if it were an enormous mousehole out of which, any moment, food was likely to appear. Every morning she made a round of the decks, looking for tiny squid or tiny flying fish (those that came aboard were the size of minnows). Finding them, she gave the growl of a saber-toothed tiger, fell on the offering, and devoured it in a moment.

She did this not from hunger but from sheer zest for fish and fishy things. We had plenty of choice cat food aboard, and each day we gave her a couple of saucers of milk made out of the powdered milk we carried aboard. These things she enjoyed, but largess from the ocean was her delight. At times, sleeping below with Kevin or Chris or Mark, Motley would wake and wonder whether a fish of some kind had not flipped onto the deck. Then, like a man who tortures himself in the middle of the night thinking of a bowl of ice cream in the refrigerator, she would at last quit her sleeping place, go on deck, and prowl around until she found some tidbit. Later in the voyage we met heavy weather and heavy seas and she was in danger of being washed overboard. Yet she became expert at judging the waves, even in the dark, and rarely got wet. Wet, she shook herself like a dog.

Motley (so called because of the variety of colors in her coat) was soon found to be infested with fleas. She was too tiny to deal with them. She spent hours scratching, and after less than a week at sea she had scratched a large part of the fur off her head and ears in her efforts to rid herself of her tormentors.

All problems on board ship are the captain's problems, and the kitten's fleas required attention from me. I therefore heated a pan of water, got out the detergent (pink, with lily of the valley scent) and put on a pair of leather gloves. I then took a firm hold of Motley and plunged her into the tub. In a moment she was all claws. That saber-toothed tiger in her ancestry came immediately to her assistance and it was all I could do to keep hold of her. I gave her a brisk rub with detergent and a good rinsing, or as good as can be given to a creature which has suddenly become a mass of writhing fish hooks, and then handed her to Mark who was waiting with a towel spread on his knees. He smothered her immediately in the towel and rubbed her, not dry but damp. And then he and Kevin, Chris, and Rick took turns picking fleas off her.

That one treatment was enough. We didn't get rid of all the fleas, but we reduced the population to a point where Motley could handle them herself. From that day forward she scratched less and less and grew fatter and fatter.

Motley, like the rest of my crew, had a movable bunk. She would crawl in with someone, and then be roused when her host had to go on watch. Then she crawled in with someone else. She never crawled in with me, however. The only privilege I had as skipper was a fixed bunk, high up—too high up for Motley to get into.

We waited now for the trades through the eighth, ninth and tenth of July. The north wind grew lighter and lighter. Our day's run fell lower and lower. On the tenth we got the spinnaker up for four hours and that night Kevin reported seeing a light fine on our port bow, ahead of us. Another, he said, had shown for a while broad on the starboard bow. We had periods of squalls followed by periods of calm. The boat was still hard to handle with the spinnaker up, particularly under the weight of a squall.

On the eleventh, the wind was very light indeed and had gone a little to the east of north. Our course was now west southwest and the trades were due to arrive at any hour; they were, in fact, three days overdue by my accounting. We kept the spinnaker up all afternoon and late into the night. Then the net broke and the spinnaker wrapped in one of those squalls which are characteristic of the approach of the trade winds. It was not a bad wrap and was undone in less than an hour. We put up the Genoa, poled out to windward, and went on our way.

By midday of the twelfth, after eight days of sailing, we had covered a thousand miles—an average of a hundred and twenty-five miles a day. Not impressive, but then there had been those first two days in which we had made only a hundred miles. That noon we got for the first time the broadcast of the rest of the racing fleet, each yacht calling in its position to that big yawl *Chiriqui* whom we had mistaken for the non-existent Point Dume light. All were ahead of us and all were heard from.

In this part of the ocean, a thousand miles offshore and four hundred miles south of the latitude of Los Angeles, we could expect to have both steady winds from the northeast and plenty of sunshine. But the winds were still northerly, at times light and at times gusty. The sky was overcast so that sun sights were rare and star sights impossible. Of one thing only was I sure and that was that we were dropping behind.

We were not pressing the boat as hard as were our competitors because of the difficulty of handling her with the spinnaker flying. This was not entirely a matter of lack of skill on our parts. We all of us tried our best, but no one was more successful than his mate. There was a point at which the spinnaker took over and the boat broached, flying across the wind and refusing to fall off even though the helm was hard over. When she did at last fall off, it was because a wave helped her.

The centerboard probably would have helped to keep her before the wind. But unfortunately the centerboard had rocked itself loose in its box and each time the ship rolled, the board, when down, banged from side to side with such force that we were afraid the hull would split. The only cure for this was to raise the board completely. That left *Cu Na Mara* with practically no underwater aid for her rudder. So she broached and taxed our strength at the wheel and made our shoulder muscles ache abominably.

Yet, if I were to do anything at all against my competitors, I had to fly that spinnaker more often. So the day after we discovered we were last, we hauled the spinnaker up again and it was hardly aloft before it took over completely. I had put the boat downwind to get the spinnaker up with the least trouble. As soon as it was full, Chris trimmed it and I let *Cu Na Mara* come back on her course. And then something happened that scared the wits out of everybody on board.

*Cu Na Mara* rounded right across the wind, which was

blowing strongly, and she was knocked flat in the water—knocked so far over that the seas started to hit her exposed bottom and I was thrown away from the wheel. The cockpit was awash and the cushions were floating about. Lying across the cockpit, with my feet in the water and the ship on her beam-ends, I grabbed the wheel and pulled it toward me. But *Cu Na Mara* could not get back on her feet. The foot of the spinnaker was in the ocean. The upper part was full of wind. The crew were clinging to the deck. Every time the ship made an effort to get up, a wave would hit her under the bilges and knock her down again.

The only way she could get upright was to get the wind out of the spinnaker. Matters were not helped any by the fact that the mainsail boom was in the water so that the sail was close inboard, which in itself prevented *Cu Na Mara* from falling off the wind.

Chris and Mark let the spinnaker sheet go but the sail was trapped in the water and nothing happened. Kevin had crawled forward to let go the spinnaker halyard. I shouted to him that I was going to let the guy loose and did so. The spinnaker pole flew forward and was brought up sharp against the forestay. The guy, rigged through the fitting in the end of the pole, pulled all the way through and the spinnaker flew out to leeward like a tent blown in half. *Cu Na Mara* got back on her feet, the spinnaker was pulled in by the sheet, and Rick, who had gone forward to help Kevin, came back into the cockpit, his face pale.

"That spinnaker pole missed Kevin's head by a fraction of an inch," he said. "He'd have been killed if it hit him."

I don't suppose that we were knocked down in the ocean for more than a few seconds. The danger, coolly viewed, was not great. But when the boat you are sailing is laid over on her beam ends by an unmanageable sail in mid-ocean and will not get back on her feet, it seems that disaster and perhaps lingering death are not far away.

In this instance all ended well. We gathered in the spinnaker and set the Genoa out to windward on the spinnaker pole. When it was done Mark said to me quite seriously, "Which would have been the best side to have jumped off of?" This was the problem which had concerned him while we lay flat in the water. I told him that as long as she floats the best thing to do is to stay with the ship.

Meanwhile, with everything tidied up, we went on with the race, still unable to use the spinnaker because of the lack of a centerboard.

# Chapter Seven

THE TRANSPAC of 1967 may go on record as being one of the chattiest ever run. I had a fine little radiotelephone on board made by the Raytheon Company and this, hooked to an insulated backstay for an antenna, gave me a surprisingly wide range for broadcast and reception. We were able to listen to the boats of the fleet reporting to *Chiriqui,* who was acting as communications center. And we soon learned that we were not the only boat which was having trouble.

That year no Coast Guard cutter was accompanying the fleet to Hawaii, which was why *Chiriqui* was handling all the calls. Tuning in one day, I picked up the tail end of a message which alerted the whole ship. The yacht *Bluebell* was in some kind of trouble. A signal had been sent to the Coast Guard and another vessel was going to her assistance.

The reports we received were scrappy, but gradually we pieced together the story. Something was the matter with her skipper. He was gravely ill and would have to be returned to California. Later came a report that he had been taken off *Bluebell* by a merchant ship and was being returned to San Diego. Later still came the report that he had reached San Diego and was hospitalized but comfortable. When we reached Honolulu we learned that he had died—the first death of the Transpac, as far as I know, in all the years of the race, though not of itself connected with the contest.

*Bluebell* was an unlucky ship that voyage. A little while after her skipper was removed, the lever operating one of her running backstays came loose and hit a crewman in the eye, inflicting so heavy a wound that for some time is was thought that he would lose the sight of one eye. *Bluebell* despite these troubles went ahead to finish the race and get a rousing reception when she got to Honolulu.

Because we couldn't keep that spinnaker up, the fleet was drawing away from us. But we heard the boats talking to the United Airlines chartered planes flying the wives of various crewmen to Hawaii and also to the *S.S. Hawaiian* of the Matson line, which was helping to relay messages. It was all very chatty and buddy-buddy and I think the big ocean freighters, crossing from San Pedro to Honolulu in six days or so, were a little envious of us for making the crossing under sail. You could almost detect the longing in the voices of the radio operators on the ships and on the planes as they contacted the racing fleet.

*Cu Na Mara* still had not found the trade winds. I apologize for harping on this point, but we were in the place where the trade winds are supposed to blow; where according to the lore of the ocean, the trade winds have been blowing since water and land first separated the one from the other. There was no trade wind blowing there. The wind was northerly, blustery in nature, building up a sharp cresting sea. The skies were still overcast and we hit a foul current, for our mileage was down to a miserable one hundred and twenty every twenty-four hours. Everybody was beginning to feel a little tired and worn, for we were nine days at sea and the work at the wheel was getting heavier as we began to experience more and more gusts. The pilot chart indicated that we were certainly at the half-way mark; in fact, beyond it.

That afternoon the winds increased and brought with them big seas rolling down off the starboard quarter. By ten in the evening we were encountering heavy squalls, making the boat extremely difficult to handle. Although we had not got the spinnaker up, and although we had the Genoa boomed out to windward, giving a very balanced sail combination, *Cu Na Mara* would get on a wave and run around across the wind and would not fall off until the Genoa had backed.

The wheel watch became an ordeal. All our strength was needed to get the wheel over and hold it there, and, wrestling with the wheel, I pulled a muscle in my shoulder which pained me for the rest of the voyage. We developed heavy calluses on our hands from the work and were at our wits ends how to make the boat more manageable.

As the weather worsened I took to reefing the main at nighttime, and on one very bad night, I took down the Genoa altogether and with a six-foot reef in the main still made five knots. For two nights we sailed in heavy seas and winds with a reefed main, unable to put up more canvas because the ship became unmanageable. The first day under this reduced rig we made a hundred and twenty-five miles. The next day we did a hundred and thirty-five miles. The following day, the wind died to a fifteen-knot breeze. We took the reef out of the main and got the spinnaker up for a few hours for I still wanted to race. That day we covered a hundred and ninety-five miles, noon to noon!

We tore through the water which boiled astern of us, leaving a wake like that of a powerboat. We were moving so fast that the transom was half buried in the ocean and only *Cu Na Mara*'s name was above water; her port of hail was submerged. A quarter-wave ran out from the corners of the transom, flinging back into the following seas and actually causing them to crest a little where they peaked.

It was hard to believe the speed of the boat. Heavy as she was to handle, she fled downwind like a stag. And even when we had to take the spinnaker down, because she was becoming unmanageable, *Cu Na Mara* still plunged on at eight knots under Genoa and main set wing and wing, and with a small cotton staysail on the same side as the mainsail.

This sail combination was as good a balance as we could get. It was now plain that wave action on her underbody was the decisive factor in whether *Cu Na Mara* broached or not. To be sure, she was most likely to broach when the wind stiffened. It was then that you could feel her start to round up to the wind, and it was then that with sinking heart you put your wheel over to correct this and hoped she would answer. There was a chance that she would answer if a wave did not catch her under the counter and swivel her around. When this happened the helm was useless. The helmsman had to wait until the Genoa backed to get the ship onto her course again.

The major consideration now was not miles per day but easing the work at the wheel. And yet we were not doing badly. One evening when the wind had lessened a little, we saw broad on our beam the eighty-three-foot ketch *Novia del Mar,* who was one of the racing fleet. She passed southward no more than a mile ahead of us and was lost as the sun set. That day, with great daring we had flown the spinnaker for four hours because the wind was lighter and, more important, the seas were easier. We covered a hundred and forty-four miles that day, and had averaged a hundred and forty miles a day for the past four days, at times with nothing but a reefed main drawing.

But there was something very, very odd about the weather. We still hadn't met a trade wind though by the evening of July 18th we were scarcely four hundred miles from Honolulu. That afternoon a mizzling rain set in. The wind went round from the north to the south in an hour and then died to a breeze. The sea flattened out and we loafed along at four knots with a fine, warm rain coming out of dirty skies.

Something, we were sure, was about to happen.

# *Chapter Eight*

THE WHOLE SKY was overcast that evening, with the clouds moving fast about us in two directions. The upper layer moved westward, but a lower stratum with a bruised and greenish tinge moved north. There was no sunset, just the disappearance of daylight and then night settled over us like a vulture. With the sun gone, the south wind died, too, and with it the rain. What was left was a lumpy sea; waves from the north meeting waves from the south, peaking up here and there and flowing over one another in such a manner as to toss *Cu Na Mara* about drunkenly.

The watch from eight to ten was mine and I could find no air anywhere to fill the mainsail which slatted about, jerking at the sheet. When an occasional breath of wind appeared and filled the sail, the lumpy sea would shake that little zephyr out of the sail and *Cu Na Mara* would make a complete circle in the ocean.

Before I handed over the wheel to Christopher at the

end of my watch, I took down all sail to stop the terrible slatting of the boom.

"If you get any wind at all, wake me up," I told him.

At midnight Kevin woke me. "There's a good strong wind making up right now," he said.

"Where from?"

"Right out of the southeast."

I went quickly on deck and we clapped on the Genoa and the main. *Cu Na Mara* started peeling off the knots, headed for the islands again. Two hours later Kevin woke me once more.

"Wind's really making up," he said. "The helm is getting very hard to handle. Rick's on the wheel and he's having trouble."

"Let's reef then," I said. Up we went and rolled a reef in the mainsail. The roller reefing gear on *Cu Na Mara* was splendid and we could reef the main almost as readily as rolling up a blind. I had hardly fallen asleep again before there came another message from the wheel. The wind was blowing even harder. Another reef was needed. We put another reef in the main, which was now not much bigger than a trysail. It still wasn't enough. *Cu Na Mara* lay over in the water, her lee rail buried, and fought her helm furiously.

The sea was now in a fury; cresting waves roaring down on us out of the darkness from the southeast. I sensed that we were in for something more than a strong blow. The motion on deck was astonishing. We were lifted swooping upward through several feet, rocked over, and let fall again only to have the same cycle repeated the next minute. It was impossible to stay on your feet. You couldn't move about above or below without holding on to lifelines and on deck we crawled. Above the thunder of the sea I heard the whine and shriek of the rigging. It was difficult to breathe in that black pandemonium and plainly we must take down all sail.

Loath to lie with naked poles in the ocean when I was supposed to be racing, we took down the Genoa first. Even under the reefed main, without headsails, *Cu Na Mara* was overpressed and hazardous to handle. I decided to ease her completely by taking down all sail and letting her lie alee in the wild and roaring wind. At dawn the sun came up in a metallic sky with mare's tails streaking out of the southeast.

Our horizon was the thundering crest of the nearest wave which, when it lifted us up, showed an ocean stretching from horizon to horizon like a snowfield with strips of blazing blue showing here and there. The sight was splendid and fearful for pandemonium was abroad over the ocean and our world filled with sounds compounded of seething and roaring seas, howling wind, and heavy thumps as we took a sea broad on our topsides.

We were, in fact, on the edge of a hurricane which had originated far south of the equator, roared across that line, and came as far north as twenty-three degrees of latitude. Everything having been made snug, the crew went below to see if they could sleep in that fury of motion and noise while I sat in the cockpit watching the sea and the sky and waiting for the wind to moderate enough to get some kind of a sail up.

Now for the first time I witnessed a classic example of the approach of a storm. I saw first the mare's tails stretching out of the storm center to the southeast. Then I saw the sheet of white cirrus spread out from the south to cover the sky, the forerunner of the fury to come. And then, and rather more to the east than the south, came the "bar" of the storm—the dark low cloud which marks the storm's center. I took a bearing on this and checked its movement. If there was no movement at all, but just an increase in size, then we were in for the full fury of the hurricane. If the bar moved, then we could with good management put the ship on a course to escape the center of the storm.

The bar was definitely moving and it was moving to the west. It was moving fast, too; in half an hour it had changed its position by several degrees. I had lashed *Cu Na Mara*'s wheel to prevent the rudder slopping about and thus being damaged. I unlashed it now and coaxed her over on the starboard tack so that she was headed northeast. On this course she was traveling away from the storm center. In that roaring sea she was making three or four knots without any canvas showing. The bar, growing in size, moved away westward, perfectly defined against the livid sky. It was very low on the horizon so the storm center could have been forty or fifty miles away. It did not change direction but kept going west. After six hours it seemed to me the wind was lessening. Having, however, now been in the wind a long time, I could not be sure whether it was going down or whether I had merely got used to it, so I called Kevin. He sat for a while in the cockpit looking about and listening and then he said, "Yes. I think it has gone down a bit."

"We could try a small sail on her," I said. "Maybe the cotton staysail." It was a favorite sail of mine, bought secondhand, made of Egyptian cotton and in excellent condition.

"We could send it up on the spinnaker halyard," said Kevin. So we unlashed it and bent it on the halyard and raised it. But it had scarcely filled stiff with wind before it split and the spinnaker halyard block on which it was being raised pulled apart, and down came the sail—half on deck and half over the side.

We gathered it in and again considered the wind. Although the sail had pulled the spinnaker halyard block apart, I didn't think that this was the result of the fury of the wind as much as wear on the block. The only other headsail I had was the Genoa, for *Cu Na Mara* had no working jib. The wind definitely seemed lessened. I particularly noted that the noise in the rigging was lower.

"Let's get the Genoa on her," I said and we started to unlash that sail. Rick had done such a good job of tying it up so it would not be swept overboard or fill with wind that we were half an hour getting the lashing off it. Up went the Genoa and *Cu Na Mara* steadied immediately, heeled under the weight of the wind, and dashed off at six knots for Honolulu. That six knots became seven when we got the Genoa trimmed right and when we added the main it rose to eight.

My sails were brand new at the start of the voyage. But when we raised the main we found that eight sail slides on the foot had come off—the thread lashing them to the foot of the sail having been broken in the slatting around the previous evening. We replaced the sail slides with individual ties, which was the way the mainsail was tied to the boom on my previous boat, *Bahia*. Then we plunged on, the speedometer often showing ten knots and rarely less than eight.

During the gale I had been doing some hard thinking. I thought about it being our fifteenth day at sea, about the very heavy work handling the wheel, about how crowded Honolulu would be with some seventy yachts arriving from the Transpac, and about my centerboard which could not be used. I also thought about the fact that we were a hundred miles closer to Hilo than to Honolulu and I had never been to Hilo. And after all this thinking I decided that we would put in at Hilo instead of Honolulu, abandoning my unofficial entry in the Transpac. So with the wind still booming out of the southeast at perhaps thirty knots, I set a course for Hilo—and then discovered, after taking a sun shot, that I couldn't lay the course.

I couldn't lay the course because I couldn't use my centerboard. We must sail close-hauled, and without her board down, *Cu Na Mara* was going sideways through the water, drifting in a line about ten degrees to leeward of the desired course according to the sextant. We got out the charts and studied them again and saw that Kahului on the island of Maui was about the same distance away as Hilo, but further off the wind. We could make Kahului with sheets started, so we laid our course for that port.

All day the wind didn't relent. From noon of the nineteenth of July to noon of the twentieth we made one hundred and eighty miles, which put Kahului only ninety miles distant.

"We will sight the island at dawn tomorrow," I said. "We should be snug in the harbor by noon."

It was Kevin's watch at dawn. The wind had blown furiously during the night, calling for a reefed main again. During my watch the boat several times swung through one hundred degrees of arc as I tried first to prevent her riding up into the wind and then, when a wave had thrown her head off, to stop her gybing as she fell off the wind and swung crazily to leeward. We had a preventer, of course, on the main boom in case she gybed and it did noble work, for there were times when the wind got on the other side of the mainsail and the boom would have come flying over but for the preventer.

Our lee deck buried time and time again as we reached

for Kahului. Water was coming in through the leeward chainplates and filling up the enclosed area at the bottom of the starboard bunk. From there it seeped over the cabin floor which was thus constantly wet.

Kevin, when he took the wheel from Rick at dawn, looked anxiously for land, but ahead were only thick mists and clouds and a wild gray sea. The wind was strong out of the southeast, a driving, merciless wind accompanied at times by rain squalls which obliterated ship, helmsman, and ocean. A little after sunrise, the thick weather lifted a little and at seven in the morning Kevin shouted, "Land! Dead ahead!"

And there it was; the slope of Haleakala, the vast volcano on the eastern end of the island of Maui. All that was to be seen immediately was a dark gray line, the color of cloud but not the shape of cloud, slipping down smoothly from the skies to the sea. We were charging down on it and soon we could distinguish a touch of color here and there—pale green and pale yellow.

The sun came out but the wind did not relent for a moment. The sea was a smother of foam and as we came closer to the island the wind backed and turned from southeast to east to northeast, so that it was almost directly behind us and driving us down on the lee shore of an island for which I had only general charts.

We looked up Kahului in the Pilot, noted the landmarks described there and strained to see them. I took the wheel and had the Genoa taken down to ease the work and slow the ship. Then we put a reef in the mainsail and, still making six knots, headed downwind toward a harbor we could not see on a coast which, to judge by the line of the breakers, was a nightmare of coral.

The boat now had to be put into such shape that she

could be maneuvered even in the press of wind if need be. That meant that the preventer had to be taken off the main boom which must be allowed to swing over to the other tack if I found that we were running into solid coral. The engine was useless for we had run out of gasoline some days before; the engine being used at that time to charge the ship's batteries, not to propel the boat. I have never yet made a strange port with an engine. We would have to make Kahului under sail, too.

The following seas made steering difficult, swinging the stern of the yacht about. Time and again she nearly gybed on me and then came the time that she did gybe. I shouted "Look out" to Rick who was in the cockpit and ducked my head. I was not quick enough. Over came the boom, hitting me a blow which knocked me to my knees. A heavy blow on the head produces curious sensations. I distinctly smelt chalk dust, wet cobwebs and, I think, furniture polish, one after another. I held onto the wheel, though, and the boom swung back again, missing me this time, and I looked at the compass. Ahead of me was the island of Maui. The compass should have read about 180 degrees—due south. Instead it read 360 degrees—due north.

I concluded that I was suffering from concussion and told Rick to take the wheel. All this, which takes so long to write, occurred in perhaps five seconds—the gybe, the blow on the head, the odd scents, and the glimpse of an island which had suddenly moved from south to north.

Rick took the wheel and I tried to steady myself by examining the cockpit floor. All seemed normal. I looked about. Sea and sky were where they should be.

"What's the course?" I asked Rick.

"South," he replied.

I looked at the compass. South it was. Then I realized

what had happened. The mainsheet had hit the binnacle as the boom went over, spinning the compass card around and I had looked at it when the card was a hundred and eighty degrees out of position. Thankful to be in my right senses, I took the wheel again.

Kevin and Mark had gone forward with the night glasses to try to spot the harbor entrance. They found the entrance buoy, but where the entrance was supposed to be, there was only a formidable breakwater of cement blocks.

Run down on that in a thirty-knot wind and a heavy following sea? It seemed to be the only thing to do. I headed for the buoy and a narrow gap opened in the breakwater around which the ocean swirled and foamed. Beyond the breakwater and to the east I could make out the spars of a big sailing ship.

"Hey, there's a full-rigged ship at anchor in there," said Kevin.

"Stand by the Genoa," I said. "We may need it to maneuver when we get in."

We shot through the harbor entrance so fast that I had only a glimpse of the concrete blocks as big as automobiles flashing by, and we were inside. I put the helm to windward and the other ship, a Japanese square-rigger, came directly before my bows. Pinching in hard I managed to set a course which would not collide with her. For a minute, all was well. And then the wind, blocked by a warehouse, headed us. The sails shivered, I fell off to get them drawing, and there was the square-rigger right in front of my bows again. We were headed for her at six knots. First one head, then two, and then a dozen popped up and peered silently over the bulwarks. Down we charged, straight for the square-rigger, until we could see the rivets in her sides. And then, with a prayer, I put the wheel upwind and *Cu Na Mara* turned prettily and headed, sails flapping, into the wind's eye. Almost with a sigh, the heads disappeared. *Cu Na Mara* ghosted upwind for two hundred yards, for the water was flat and she had been traveling fast, and Kevin had the anchor rigged and ready. The Genoa came down and as soon as she started to fall back, Kevin let the anchor go. Mark and Christopher brought down the mainsail and *Cu Na Mara* lay unbelievably motionless in the mirror-quiet.

Two thousand miles in sixteen days and ten hours, two of them days of flat calm.

"Let's go ashore and get a hamburger," said Christopher.

# Chapter Nine

WE WOULD NOT have done brilliantly had we been racing officially. On the other hand, we would not have been the last boat in. On corrected time, I think we would have come in somewhere in the tail end of the fleet.

We went ashore and got a battery charged and bought some gasoline and ate some food and I got a decent cup of coffee and we found a laundromat in which to launder our salt-drenched clothing. We rented a car and for two days we forgot about *Cu Na Mara* and explored Maui, certainly one of the most enchanting of the Hawaiian group.

Mark announced that he had an uncle living in Lahaina on the other side of the island. He called him and we piled into the car and went to make the acquaintance of Wally Boskoff and his wife Laura. They gave us more coffee and good things to eat and after a little while the land stopped rocking and began to look a little more real. Wally said he could find us a slip at Lahaina, which is on the leeward side of Maui, and we had better get in there before some of the

Transpacers came down that way visiting. Kevin, Chris, and Mark found a surfboard and Rick and I were given to understand that we must bring the boat around to Lahaina from Kahului alone.

The journey was uneventful except for one astonishing occurrence. Not wishing to have any more struggles at the wheel, I elected to sail with the Genoa only, and with the engine running to give us a push. There was the usual brisk wind off the island outside the harbor and a rather big swell running in; but it was nothing compared with the waves of the outer ocean. We were dry and warm and Rick had the wheel while I basked in the pleasant sun in thoroughly dry clothing.

And then, without the slightest warning, a huge sea rose in the ocean and climbed aboard *Cu Na Mara*. It did not lift her up. It did not push her aside. It just materialized and swamped the whole boat, filling the cockpit and drenching Rick and me to our necks. Those lovely, dry, sweet-smelling, soft clothes were in an instant sopping wet. The lovely, dry cockpit was in an instant a bathtub of cold water. And then, its prank played, the ocean abated, and for the rest of the voyage, we sailed around the west end of Maui and to Lahaina, which was once a whaling port and said to be the place where surfing began, and which is a nice, snug little harbor in which to lie after an ocean crossing.

Wally took us exploring up a river which flowed out of the lovely mountains of Maui and we swam in a pool under a waterfall which came roaring down from the rocks above. We went up that river until we were in the clouds and a gentle rain fell around us, while below the sun shone brightly on the lowlands. Carved in the rocks we saw the petroglyphs of the Hawaiians, which meant nothing to us but had undoubtedly meant much to them. And we returned so tired that we could scarcely move.

Hazel flew out from California to join us and we rested from the sea and explored the island, still ignoring the boat. I did, however, dive off *Cu Na Mara* with a faceplate, and found that some of the epoxy around the centerboard housing had been broken by the banging of the board against the sides, and also that the lower gudgeon or hinge for the rudder was loose—so loose that I could shake it by hand.

We did a few ship-keeping jobs, restored those sail slides on the main, tightened up the lifelines, got that water which had come in through the chainplates out from underneath the starboard bunk, charged the batteries, and hosed out belowdecks.

We had to keep poor little Motley aboard all the time, for there was a very heavy fine payable if she landed on the islands. She was a kitten with some of the characteristics of a dog, resulting, perhaps, from the lack of maternal guidance. Not only did she growl when presented with fresh fish, but she took to jumping over the side and swimming to other boats if we were visiting them. Her mother had not told her that cats avoid water. She made a bed for herself in the mainsail and lived in her snow palace happily, now and again, however, eyeing the ocean from which came such lovely and unexpected gifts of fish. She was a great favorite in the harbor, where we soon had plenty of company as one by one the Transpac fleet started dropping into Lahaina preparatory to starting the return voyage to California.

*Holiday II,* that year's overall winner, was moored alongside us. Close by was the black-hulled fifty-foot yawl *Bat* and then *Simoon,* another fifty-footer. Next, light and graceful and long, came *Stormvogel,* and with her *Audacious.* We learned we were not the only boat to have had rough handling. *Salacia* had lost a mast in one of the squalls on the approach to the islands. *Rampage* had had trouble with her rudder and she had rolled so abominably that one or two of her crew were so seasick they were incapacitated and had had to be taken off by a Coast Guard cutter.

Talking with the other crews we found several of the boats had been knocked down as we had, and many had had steering troubles with their spade rudders, a design which, like the calendar, has not yet been perfected. I was beginning to wonder how to get *Cu Na Mara* back to California when I discovered I had to return there urgently myself by air as a result of an occurrence which has no relationship to this book.

Back in California, it seemed to me that the best thing to do was to ship *Cu Na Mara* home on a barge and have her repaired at a local shipyard. And so I wrote and told Kevin to take her up to Honolulu for shipment and sent air fares home for my crew, and determined to forget about ocean racing.

Do you recall the tale of the sailor who was utterly disenchanted with the sea, and who therefore put an oar across his shoulder and started to walk inland? When, after several days of travel inland, someone asked him what was the curious object he was carrying on his shoulder, he decided that he was now far enough from the ocean to settle down in safety.

Such was my mood when I got back to California and sent for *Cu Na Mara*. I was through with boats and through with ocean racing. I took to going to sports stores and looking at bags of golf clubs. I handled a tennis racket or two and inquired diffidently about the price of polo ponies, and stayed firmly away from the yacht harbor for several weeks.

# *Chapter Ten*

AT THIS POINT, if you are not already a sailor, I should warn you gravely against exposure to sailing. It is a contagious disease of remarkable virulence. Some are certainly immune to it, but those who are not, and who contract it, cannot be cured. The disease will at times abate, to be sure. It will go through periods of quiescence and it may even produce symptoms which suggest the direct opposite of the affliction—namely, a hatred of boats, burgees, flags, halyards, charts, compasses, and westerly winds. But it will always return and the victim, once afflicted, can be cured only by death—and I am not sure about death.

Peter, for instance. Can you imagine him very far away from the water, even now? Surely there is still around him a faint aroma of tarred rope, and his clothes must often be wet from handling a net or a flogging sail. And what of Magellan or Drake or Vasco da Gama? Can you really believe that their eyes do not light a little when the wind stiffens out of the northeast and the heavenly trees lean like tall ships in the clean wind?

No, love of sailing is an incurable affliction and the old seamen spoke truly when they said that it is easier to swallow the anchor than to turn your back upon the ocean.

I, however, turned my back on it for two whole months. I avoided the company of my fellow yachtsmen and turned to worthier occupations, such as mowing the lawn and raising roses. For twenty years I have tried to raise an orange in California and failed. But now, the sea at last behind me, I sprayed my dwarf orange tree at the right time and watered it at the right time, and the fruit set, and five small oranges promised to come to fullness.

Then came a telephone call with the news that a barge had arrived in San Diego with *Cu Na Mara* on board and I had better come down and fetch her.

Even then I didn't want to get her. If I could have arranged without expense for someone else to get her and bring her up to Portofino, I believe I would have embraced the arrangement. But I had to get her, so I went down to San Diego with Kevin and Mark and found the barge in the maze of docks. There were a number of other boats on board the barge, for not all the Transpacers sailed their yachts back from Hawaii.

I arrived just before the longshoremen were due to unload *Cu Na Mara*. "You want her in the water or on the dock?" asked the foreman.

"In the water," I said.

"Cost you another fifty bucks," said the foreman. The dock was on one side of the barge and the water was on the other side. But that's the way it is with yachts, as Commodore Vanderbilt said.

Up to this point I could not see *Cu Na Mara*. She was

somewhere behind the huge bulwark of the barge. A few shouts were exchanged between the men on the barge and the operator of a crane and the boom of the crane came down. Two slings hung loose from the end of the boom and were taken by the men on board the barge. A few seconds later *Cu Na Mara* rose in the air, and my heart skipped a beat. She was the most beautiful thing I have ever seen in my life. She had lines like a shark of the upper classes. She could lick anything that ever floated on the water, including the *Cutty Sark*. She looked proud but a little bruised and awfully glad to see me.

They put her in the water and I went on board almost with tears in my eyes. I had sea fever all over again. Her masts were lying on horses across the length of her and she looked as though she hadn't had a mumbling word from a soul who knew her for a month.

I forgot all about the wicked helm and about being knocked down and about every other thing that had happened and gave her a little pat, and I think some of the loneliness went out of her right then. We got the cabin open and poured some gasoline in the tanks; turned on the blower and fired up the engine. And that engine started right away. (That it stalled as soon as we had pulled away from the dock and were helpless in mid-channel merely proved that it was a marine engine; they always stall at the worst time.)

And so I was reunited with *Cu Na Mara* and set about healing her hurts. I contacted the Morgan Yacht Corporation at Fort Lauderdale, Florida. The upshot of our correspondence was that they sent out their plant manager to examine *Cu Na Mara* and following his examination they agreed to pay the whole cost of the repairs and half of my out-of-pocket expenses in fetching *Cu Na Mara* back by barge; and they were as good as their word.

The lower gudgeon on the rudder was refastened and two neoprene "cheek" pieces installed on each side of the centerboard. These did not prevent the centerboard from knocking from side to side in a sea trial so we brought *Cu Na Mara* back to the shipyard and installed marine bronze bearing plates on both sides of the board, reaching up as far into the centerboard box as could be contrived. That did the trick.

For all this work the Morgan Company paid and offered to do other small things as well; such as reseal the area around the chainplates where the water came through the deck, and reseal the plexiglass on the forehatch which had leaked slightly. But I regarded such leaks as part of the normal wear and tear on a boat and was well satisfied with the fixing of the centerboard and the rudder. And then, with *Cu Na Mara* restored and her bottom paint touched up, I looked around for a coastal race or two in which to enter her and try her out.

The first that offered was on a most propitious day for me, March 17, 1968, Saint Patrick's Day. Since we were approaching the spring equinox, we could expect a good wind and we got one. We got handily across the starting line at the weather end which was important on this course for the first leg lay to windward. There were twenty-six contestants in our class, the greater part of them sloops of about the same size as *Cu Na Mara,* including several Cal 34s which are reckoned to be the fastest or among the fastest of the thirty-four-foot sloops in this part of the world. In a light breeze *Cu Na Mara* has a neutral helm, rather like a powerboat, and Kevin is a better helmsman than I in these circumstances. We started in such a breeze, but the wind picked up as each hour passed, and when we got to the windward mark, we were flying.

It is surprising how, in such races, all the yachts are

crowded together at the starting line and then half an hour later they are scattered about the ocean and scarcely to be found. I thought we were doing badly, for I could see none of our class around, but at the windward mark the others started to congregate—three Cal 34s and a Columbia 34. I was able to hold to the starboard tack, claim right of way, and get around before them. There followed a close reach in which I lost a little ground because I needed a bigger Genoa. And then a run off the wind for which Kevin got the spinnaker set without fuss and, with our centerboard up, we pulled ahead of the competition. Since the Cal 34s had to give us handicap time we could still beat them if they were a little ahead of us. Being in the middle of them, we were doing very well indeed.

The wind had now increased to perhaps twenty knots or a trifle more. On the close-hauled leg (for we were to go twice around the course) I decided to reef the main, for the boat seemed overpressed. We reefed quickly for *Cu Na Mara*'s roller reefing gear is among the superior inventions of mankind. We reefed while sailing and immediately a Cal 34 behind us, unreefed, and over on her ears and floundering along like a swan with a broken wing, went right past us. I stubbornly stuck to the reef, and we finished last.

It was not as black as it sounds, however, for out of the twenty-six who started, only six finished and none of them were Cal 34s. Boat for boat, we beat a Columbia 34, but having to give her time on handicap, she readily beat us. The revealing part of that race, however, came in the journey of ten miles back to my slip in Portofino Harbor. The westerly blew harder and harder. It was broad on our beam since my course home was to the south. Short, steep, fast-moving seas, the walls glittering like glass in the sunlight, built up quickly and drenched us all. The harder the wind blew, the more difficult it was to handle the helm. There were times when *Cu Na Mara* would not answer her helm at all, but rode around into the wind until knocked off by one of those glittering seas. In short, even with the centerboard working, *Cu Na Mara* still had that weather helm we had fought all the way to Hawaii. This would not do at all. If the boat was to be of any use to me, that weather helm had to be cured.

When, soaking wet, we got back home at last, I called Bill Crealock, a well-known naval architect who had inspected the boat for me on her return from Hawaii, and I told him about the helm. "Any suggestions?" I asked.

"I don't guarantee anything but you might try increasing her rudder size to start with," said Bill.

"How much?" I asked.

"Increase it by about thirty percent," said Bill. "Not on the trailing edge. As close to the axis as you can. In other words, make it deeper. You might try balancing it a bit by having a small portion of the increase ahead of the axis."

"I'll let you know what happens," I said and hung up. I took the boat down to the San Pedro Boat Works and talked the problem over with John Leeper, the yard superintendent.

The problem of increasing the efficiency of the rudder of a boat was not new to John. That problem is common to almost all modern yacht designs, particularly those with spade rudders. The main reason I think is that many designs are really in a testing stage. Every effort is undoubtedly made to perfect them before they are put on the market; but lines laid down on paper and tests performed in the still water of tanks cannot foretell everything that is going to happen in every condition of wind and wave. Testing tanks give copious information on how water flows past a particular hull design. They say nothing about how the hull is affected when the water is pushing up from astern or off the quarter in the form of waves. Testing tanks can demonstrate the efficiency of a hull at particular angles of heel; but no boat under sail is at a particular angle of heel—it swings through a great number of angles in the course of a minute—through them and back again. So the real test is the performance of the boat at sea.

*Cu Na Mara* had been given that test across two thousand miles of ocean. The findings were that she needed a bigger rudder and John Leeper looked at her when she was hauled and nodded his head sagely for he had done that job on many other boats.

I gave him a sketch showing my proposal for increasing the rudder area by thirty percent. He looked it over and illustrated his own ideas on the rudder blade with a piece of yellow chalk. We compromised and John said, with that quizzical look of his, "We'll have to take the rudder off to do this job properly."

"Just bear in mind that the rumor that I own the Bank of England is untrue," I said.

A week later the work was done, the rudder had been lengthened and built up on its forward edge and slightly balanced. The bill, Commodore, was three hundred and seventy-nine dollars.

# Chapter Eleven

AROUND ABOUT THIS time, that is to say the end of March, 1968, the ocean racing fever began to assert itself once more. I had twice attempted to enter an ocean yacht race and twice my plans had come to nothing. But now I heard of a race for smaller boats from California to Hilo, on the island of Hawaii (there are several Hawaiian Islands, but only the biggest of them all is named Hawaii). *Cu Na Mara* had failed to make the Transpac the previous year because she was too small. It seemed that she would certainly qualify for this contest which was called the Little Transpac, so I wrote asking for an entry form. But the race was cancelled, for the difficulties of organization proved too great.

Then, leafing through a magazine I found an item about a race from Victoria, British Columbia, to Lahaina, that same port on the island of Maui in the Hawaiian group at which *Cu Na Mara* had stayed for some weeks the previous year.

From Hermosa Beach to Victoria, B. C., is a distance of well over a thousand miles. It is a long sail to get to the starting line. On the other hand, this seemed to be the only long-distance race for which *Cu Na Mara* could qualify. (She had been ruled out of the one other race—to Mazatlán in Mexico—because she was not big enough.) If I was going to get into an ocean race at all and die happy, it looked like the Victoria-Maui event was my only chance. I wrote a one-line letter asking for an entry form. In double quick time the entry blank had been sent to me, together with a list of requirements for competing yachts.

I looked over the list and it was all familiar, almost the same requirements as those which I had already fulfilled not once but twice for the Transpac. This was the point at which I could either get out of the race or get in. In a state pretty close to hypnosis I filled out the entry blank and mailed it off with my check for the entry fee. And I was in. Actually I never really had a chance. My reason might tell me that it was nonsense to enter a race which started so far away; but my nature would have nothing to do with my reason and won the day.

The first thing to do was to get a Cruising Club of America certificate for *Cu Na Mara.* This would provide her with one of those mystical numbers with which she would be handicapped. I had been through this procedure with *Bahia,* and I called Bill Steele the measurer again and made an appointment for the boat to be measured. Since *Cu Na Mara* would have to be physically weighed I made an appointment for this to be done at the Cabrillo Boat Works where they had a sling that could pick her up out of the water and put her back down again.

Everything went off well. Bill went through his ritual of floating those pieces of wood in the water and measuring certain vital distances from them. And with her water tanks and her gasoline tanks emptied, with her sails and the stipulated amount of food on board, with an inflatable life raft (borrowed) in her lazaret, her mast unstepped and laid on the deck, and all in apple pie order, *Cu Na Mara* was picked up in the sling and proved to weigh, in racing trim, 12,510 pounds.

Just as she was about to be put down in the water again, I glanced at her rudder, which represented, as I remarked before, about two sets of golf clubs, or a fine pair of snow skis and boots, and noticed that the antifouling paint around the lower gudgeon was cracked. I motioned to the operator of the crane to hold her a moment and reached over and took hold of that gudgeon. I was horrified. It was so loose I could shake it with my fingers.

But how could it be loose? It had been taken off. It had been refastened. Sleeves had been put into the bolt holes to make sure the fastenings were tight. An extra fastening had been added. And there it was loose after perhaps forty miles of sailing.

As soon as I had the mast stepped I took her around the corner to the San Pedro Boat Works and looked up John Leeper.

"Let's haul her and take a look at her," he said. And so we did. It was then that we discovered that the rudder shaft was not continuous through the rudder. It entered the rudder at the top and ended perhaps midway through. The bottom portion was a separate piece. And the bottom and the top portions were not on center with each other. This meant that when the rudder was turned from side to side, the bottom post, having a different center, had to go through a wider circle than the top. And in doing that it had to shake that bottom gudgeon loose. So the looseness of that gudgeon when I got to Hawaii was not the result of excessive strain on the rudder as I had supposed, but rather of the bottom portion of the rudder post being off-center. And this accounted for a certain slight groaning, both felt and heard, in moving the wheel from side to side, which I had thought was the result of inadequate lubrication somewhere in the steering mechanism.

The rudder had to be pulled again. You are quite right, Commodore Vanderbilt. A mere nothing. In fact, only $332.35 or maybe two sets of golf clubs with grips of black all-weather rubber and gold color trim. On the other hand, I had at this point spent $711.35 on just getting a rudder adequate to the boat and one that would turn without binding from side to side. I paid the bill without flinching and when I was well out of sight of the shipyard on my way back to Hermosa, I lay down in the bottom of the cockpit and had a good cry.

I couldn't see, however, that there were many other big expenses ahead in preparing for the race. I tried to avoid thinking about sails by assuring myself that one spinnaker, a Genoa, and a main, all just a year old, were adequate. Which was nonsense. Eventually I decided that I ought to buy a spinnaker staysail and a storm spinnaker. The spinnaker staysail, in green and white panels, cost $145. The storm spinnaker, in blue and gold, cost $475.85. The blue and gold was by no means my idea. I wanted green and white, but all the sailmaker had was blue and gold, take it or leave it, so I took it. It was a lovely spinnaker of 2.2 ounce nylon. It looked strong enough to pull the mast clean out of the boat and it did a little to cheer me up as my bank balance dwindled.

There would not be, I thought, much else to buy. I was wrong, of course. The shark repellent I had bought for

*Bahia* was lost so I had to buy more. And so was the sea dye. And the man-overboard-lights wouldn't work and had to be replaced. Also I had to buy two of those horseshoe life rings approved by the Coast Guard, and with their stands they cost me a hundred and fifty dollars. A third life ring had to be provided to lie close to the helmsman and that was another fifty dollars. The litany went on and on. Not a dollar here and a dollar there at all. It was twenty dollars here and thirty dollars there, justifying the saying that a yachtsman is someone who stands in his best clothes under a cold shower and passes the time by tearing up fifty-dollar bills.

Reading through the equipment list for the race I paid special attention this time to the question of the life raft. I thought I had this matter solved, but I hadn't. A special life raft was required. It had to be self-inflating. It had to carry six men. It had to be packed in a container. It had to have a self-erecting canopy over it. And it had to be equipped with a sea anchor, a bellows or hand inflation pump, a signaling torch, three approved handflares, three parachute flares, a bailer, a repair kit, two paddles, a safety knife, a rescue quoit and line, a first-aid kit, a small gaff, two strong fishing lines and six hooks, three sealed lifeboat cans of fresh water, and a "reasonable supply of emergency food rations similar to those used by . . . U.S. Navy in aircraft life rafts."

I began calling up friends, acquaintances and perfect strangers begging the loan or hire of such a raft. I could not find one. I inquired into the price. There was only one supplier in the United States. His premises were in Florida and his price was four hundred and fifty dollars—for the raft. You supply the flares, fishing lines and so on.

I gritted my teeth and ordered the raft. I consoled myself that at least in taking *Cu Na Mara* by sea, on her own bottom, up the coast, I would be saving some money. I went carefully over the racing budget (a large part of it an advance against a book to be written on the subject of ocean racing). It was all gone. It had been swallowed up in paying for the rudder, the spinnaker, the spinnaker staysail, the raft, and the shark repellent. I was now on my own. I didn't even have money in my budget to buy stores and gasoline for taking the boat up the coast. But I wasn't going to quit now—not with all that money already spent.

My problems so far had concerned the boat, but there were others concerning her crew. I knew Kevin would come with me, though he would not be available for the voyage up the coast, he would join the ship in Vancouver. Christopher wanted to play baseball (at which he is very good) during the summer and so would not be signing on. Rick Flewellin had left again under sail for Hawaii and was not available. Mark had to stay home. I rounded up a number of recruits, but one by one they were eliminated by various factors. One was called up to go into the Coast Guard—after waiting for two years to get in. Another became ill, and so on.

In desperation I recalled two lifeguards at Hermosa Beach who earlier in the year had determined to row from California to New York in a dory; an attempt in which they had been defeated. Two such young men, I was sure, would make excellent crewmen for a trans-ocean race. But I was too late—thirsting for adventure, they had both joined the Marines and were now in Vietnam.

At the lifeguard station, however, I was put in touch with a young man from Tasmania, Rob Barret, who was at loose ends and looking for something to do until the Olympic Games opened in Mexico. I contacted him and he agreed to join my crew immediately, although warning me that he knew nothing whatever about sailing. He had a good, adventurous spirit, so that his lack of knowledge about sailing didn't bother me—spirit being more important in my view than mere technique. I found one other young man who would crew up to Victoria but could not crew from Victoria to Maui on the race, having other engagements.

That was as good as I could do. I loaded *Cu Na Mara* down with stores and gasoline, paid her last bills, bought a radio direction finder on credit and pushed off. We had ten days in which to get to Victoria, and I figured a hundred miles a day would readily put us there in time for the starting gun. Of course when we arrived, I would have to find three more crewmen. But after all the difficulties already overcome that didn't seem monstrous.

We didn't get very far. Thirty miles up the coast we ran into fog so dense that the bow of the boat disappeared. At two in the morning I sat at the wheel considering all those cans of food we had stowed below and considering the accuracy of my compass. Cans of food are picked up these days by magnetic cranes so all cans are magnetized. It was entirely possible that my compass was not accurate. It could be several degrees east or west of magnetic north in its reading.

On my starboard was the mainland of California and somewhere on my port bow should be Anacapa Island and then Santa Cruz. Somewhere ahead in the fog was the bow of my boat but I could not see it. I was traveling one of the busiest shipping lanes on the West Coast, with ships converging from all directions on San Pedro, and heavy coastwise traffic coming down from San Francisco and points north. Every now and then *Cu Na Mara* would rock violently in the wake of some ship plunging unseen to port or starboard. I stuck it out for four hours and concluded that this was not seamanship but idiocy—the equivalent of going for a stroll on a freeway in the middle of the night.

I turned around on the reciprocal of my course and headed back for Hermosa Beach. An hour later I touched a sandbar off Zuma Beach, proof enough that my compass was off. I came back into Portofino Harbor next day to learn that two freighters, each armed with radar, had collided at sea four miles from my position, one having sliced the bow off the other.

The fog, the weather bureau reported, extended to within a few miles of San Francisco and for forty miles off the coast. It was likely to last several days.

There was now only one way to get *Cu Na Mara* to the starting line in Victoria in time for the race, and that was by truck. I started telephoning and found that truck rates varied enormously. I had heard that shipment by sea might be cheaper than by road but this was not the case. Shipment by rail was well over fifty percent more expensive than by truck. I finally got hold of the Boat Transit Company in Newport Beach. They would take *Cu Na Mara* to Anacortes, Washington, a small town across the Strait of Juan de Fuca from Victoria for a sum sufficient to buy six of those sets of golf clubs with the all-weather black leather-like grip. They would supply a cradle for her as well.

We had a great struggle with the cradle. *Cu Na Mara,* having no keel, required a cradle of a peculiar shape and the cradle brought to take her did not fit at all. We discovered this when she was out of the water, hanging from a sling on a crane. The cradle had then to be cut to size. At this point, the truck driver, Pete Rios, took over. Making cradles for boats was no part of his job, but he got a saw, a hammer, and a drill and under Pete's supervision we redesigned the cradle, cut it to pieces, and bolted it back together again. The work took six hours of the hottest day in the history of San Pedro. We had only a handsaw to cut through pieces of four-by-four and we had to work fast for *Cu Na Mara* was costing money while hanging in that crane.

Finally the cradle was made and *Cu Na Mara* lowered into it. The cradle groaned a trifle, but did not sag or collapse. Pete drove down the road with the boat on his truck and Rob and I drove behind him (for Rob had remained with me and was overjoyed that we were to race after all) to see if there was any danger of the boat falling off that makeshift cradle. She sat firmly on it, however, and I waved to Pete that all was well. The next time I saw *Cu Na Mara* was at Anacortes.

Meanwhile there was still that very disturbing question of crew. The rules of the race demanded a minimum of five on board. I had three—Kevin, Rob, and myself. I called the secretary of the race in Victoria, Mr. E. E. Curtis, who was no relation to the Mr. Gordon Curtis who had been in charge of the arrangements for the Transpac the previous year. He suggested a young Englishman in Vancouver living aboard a large ketch, *Mir,* which was to have competed in the same race, but had suffered the loss of her whole sail wardrobe in a warehouse fire. The Englishman's name was George Greenwood.

I called him and we had a ridiculous little conversation, in view of the matter concerned. I asked him whether he had any spinnaker experience. He said he had some but was by no means an expert. I asked him about racing and he said he had raced in England and was a member of the Royal Ocean Racing Club. Since one doesn't become a member of the Royal Ocean Racing Club without considerable experience, I asked him whether he would like to crew on *Cu Na Mara* to Lahaina.

He said he would, and I agreed to meet him in Anacortes. And that was that. I also sent him a list of groceries I would need for the boat and a money order for two hundred dollars with which to buy them. The money arrived but not the list—or at least not until very much later.

I now had four crewmen and needed one more. Nobody offered in my own part of the world, so I called Mr. Curtis again. And he suggested a Mr. Dan O'Brien of Seattle, Washington, and gave me his telephone number. I called up Mr. O'Brien and we had about the same conversation Mr. Greenwood and I had had. At the end of our talk, I had my crew of five. I took on a sixth crewman in Victoria; Bob Edwards, a sixteen-year-old Canadian with considerable experience on cruising boats and one enormously important talent—he could shin up the mast.

And so at last we were complete. We flew to Anacortes, located *Cu Na Mara,* got her mast restepped and the stores on board and the crew together and the water tanks filled and the gas tanks filled, and, taking her over to Victoria, attended all the pre-race meetings we could in the enormous Empress Hotel in Victoria. Then came the first of July and the start of my first ocean race.

# *Chapter Twelve*

THE DISTANCE OF the race from Victoria, British Columbia, to Lahaina, Maui, Hawaiian Islands, was officially set at 2,310 miles. That, of course, was only a figure from which handicaps would be worked out. The distance sailed by individual boats might be several hundred miles more for it would almost certainly prove impossible to head directly for Lahaina. The best strategy obviously would be to sail the shortest distance possible, at the fastest speed that could be attained.

How simple that is—and how complicated. Because, to do so it would be necessary to judge where to catch the winds and sail fast, and where to miss the calms and avoid loss of time. We were to receive a daily weather broadcast giving in code barometric pressures over a vast area of the northern Pacific. By linking these barometric pressures together a wind pattern would emerge for our guidance or distress.

Between us and Hawaii lay one huge trap—a weather system called the North Pacific High. Here was a windless or nearly windless area, of varying size and uncertain position somewhere in our path. This area must be avoided at all costs, for to fall into it would be to lose the race. All the talk in the days before the race among all skippers and crews tended to concentrate on avoiding the North Pacific High, which assumed the character of an ogre, groping blindly about the ocean to seize whatever craft came within its clutches.

There actually wasn't that much talk boat to boat, however. A sort of secrecy descended on us, arising out of rivalry, for we all, I am sure, had evolved brilliant plans for getting to Hawaii first. We looked at each other with the cold but polite eyes of gentlemen about to engage in a duel. In conversation we made only offhand remarks of no consequence at all. We looked at each other's boats and withheld comment except of the most trivial kind. And we secretly pondered the North Pacific High, which expanded and contracted somewhere in the ocean, and moved east and then south and then west, menacing all.

For myself, I evolved a brilliant and simple plan for winning the race. I decided that I would sail *Cu Na Mara* as fast as I could in whatever wind offered and in the general direction of Lahaina. But my main consideration would be to keep moving at a good speed, so that if I could lay the direct course at five knots, but a course a point or two off that line at seven knots, then I would sail the greater distance but at the higher speed. Second to this, I decided, for the first few days I would head generally south southwest until I got to 30 North and 138 West where, the wind charts issued by the United States Hydrographic Office said, I could expect to meet strong trades in July.

That course should take me clear of the North Pacific High and give me a run with the trades on my starboard quarter direct for Lahaina. We expected to fetch Lahaina in fourteen days but in compliance with the rules, had food and water for three weeks at sea.

There were fourteen contestants in the race, divided into three classes. Largest was Her Majesty's Canadian Ship *Oriole,* a magnificent ninety-one-foot ketch, Lieutenant Commander G. S. Hilliard commanding. She came into Victoria the day of the race, dressed in bunting and a lovely sight. But she had only a slight chance of winning for her handicap was enormous and she would need heavy winds indeed to reach her hull speed.

With her, in Class I, was *Porpoise III* owned by F. R. Killam and designed by Peter Hatfield with the Victoria-Maui Race in mind, according to the program. She was a lovely thing, very modern and looking very fast. Then came *Gabrielle III,* a Sparkman and Stephens design, almost fifty-four feet overall and scarcely a year old. She was owned by P. R. Sandwell and had a crew of seven plus her owner. Then John H. Long's graceful *Mary Bower,* an older forty-nine-foot sloop with the characteristic English look of length and depth. I judged she would do well to windward but would not surf downwind—and this was largely a downwind race. *Velaris,* a forty-seven-foot sloop owned by L. H. Killam, who was a brother to the owner of *Porpoise III* and would skipper her to Lahaina, was the last Class I boat.

There were five boats in Class II. *Moonglow III* was a Cal 40 owned and skippered by D. D. Nielsen. *African Star,* a lovely wooden William Atkin-designed cutter, thirty-five feet overall, was skippered by her owner D. M. Fryer. She had a bowsprit and was a joy to see with a look about her that reminded me of eighteenth-century Bristol, Long John Silver, and the Spyglass Tavern. Then, D. J. Lawson's *Cubara,* a new Sparkman and Stephens design; *Potlatch II,* built by her skipper-owner W. G. Meakes and a very fine piece of work too; and *Tiffany,* a yawl of just over forty feet owned by D. Angus and sporting a spinnaker with a diamond ring as its emblem.

In Class III, the smallest class in both number of entries and size of boats, there were only four of us. *Jeunesse* belonged to P. T. Cote, who had won the Lipton Cup with her in 1966. Then came *Rainbird,* the only schooner in the race, being an adaptation of a Gloucester fisherman. She was designed by William Garden for his own use and would be skippered by her owner, William B. Johnson. *Suerte,* a new yawl built to a design of Philip Rhodes and skippered by Q. H. Gardner, was the smallest entry in the race. And then *Cu Na Mara,* whose sole claim to distinction lay in that she had come the farthest to be present at the starting line—though on a truck.

We on *Cu Na Mara* were mostly interested in the other three boats in our class: *Rainbird, Jeunesse,* and *Suerte.* We had to give time to *Suerte* but the other two had to give time to us. A secondary consideration were the other boats in the fleet, for there was a handsome prize to be had for coming in first overall on corrected time. Theoretically, on the handicap system, any boat properly handled and sailed to her fullest could win that prize. I confess that while aboard *Moonglow III,* munching sandwiches very kindly provided by Skipper D. D. Nielsen and his wife, *Moonglow III*'s navigator, I entertained quite uncharitable thoughts of beating her not merely on corrected time but boat for boat. But that was not because I didn't like the kindly Nielsens; but because I belong to that group of yachtsmen who are bound and determined to stamp out Cal 40s because Cal 40s are too successful.

Of the boats entered five were American: *African Star,*

*Moonglow III*, *Rainbird*, *Suerte*, and *Cu Na Mara*. We were treated with great warmth and kindness. *Cu Na Mara* was adopted by an English family, the Eatons. They visited the boat several times and brought us, before our departure, both their good wishes and an excellent cake and some jam. The arrangements of the race committee under the direction of the excellent Mr. E. E. Curtis could not be bettered. And on the first of July, at nine in the morning, we all left our berths in the middle of the city of Victoria—surely no city in the world has such lovely docking facilities for visiting yachts, right in the middle of the splendid town—and headed for the starting line.

At that moment, finally able to start an ocean race, my mouth felt so dry I could scarcely swallow. The wheel felt quite strange in my hands. "Get the main on her," I said, and reflected that for two weeks, day and night, that sail would be at work. I hoped, as I watched it go up on the halyard, that it would last.

# *Chapter Thirteen*

OWING SO MUCH already to the sage advice of Commodore Vanderbilt of revered memory, I decided to use a Vanderbilt start for the Victoria–Maui Race. This is a very simple method of getting over the line right after the signal is given. First, I established the speed of my boat sailing away from the line, and then I established the speed of my boat sailing for the line—and the windward end.

It fell out that I could sail to the line a trifle faster than I could sail away from it. We were to be given two warning signals before the start itself, scheduled for ten A.M. The first warning signal, the firing of a gun and the raising of a white flag, would be ten minutes before the start. The second, the firing of a gun and the raising of a blue signal, would be five minutes before the start. The start would come with the firing of the gun and the raising of a red signal. The good Commodore, who had many times been confronted with these same circumstances, had devised a method of sailing away from the starting line for a certain number of minutes and then tacking (or gybing) and heading for the starting line with just enough minutes left to bring him across the line, flying, as the start was signaled.

In my case, having timed myself on several occasions from the starting line on an easterly course for two and a half minutes and then back to the starting line on a westerly course for two and a half minutes, I found that all would be well if I got to the starting line five minutes before the start, sailed away from it for two and a half minutes, tacked (losing thirty seconds on the tack) and then headed back for the line. I gave Rob the stopwatch and had him practice using it, for they are panicky things if you are not completely familiar with them. We were on the line as the five-minute flag went up. Over went the wheel and we headed away in a lovely easterly, with *Porpoise III* and *Velaris* a little upwind of us and a little behind. "One minute," cried Rob. "Two minutes . . . two minutes thirty seconds . . ."

"Stand by to tack," I cried and put the wheel upwind. Over came *Cu Na Mara* and round, too, went *Porpoise III* and *Velaris*. They had the wind a little freer than I, but we hit the line in that order: *Porpoise III, Velaris, Cu Na Mara.*

Across the line, the wind now being aft, the thing to do was to raise a spinnaker. Here we did not do so well. We were largely strangers to each other and had had only the briefest spinnaker drill. We were fifteen minutes getting that spinnaker set and in that time we had fallen to the tail of the fleet. *Jeunesse* went by with a spinnaker and a spinnaker staysail drawing. *Rainbird,* the Gloucester schooner, came up under our lee and sailed on through, reaching well. And when the spinnaker was at last set on *Cu Na Mara,* the morning easterly died and a sullen glassiness descended on the Strait of Juan de Fuca.

We had ebb tide, and Dan O'Brien, who knew these waters, said the smart thing to do was to get over to the American shore, three or four miles away, for the tide ebbed faster over there and when it came in, its flow was weaker than on the Canadian side of the Strait.

For the time being we couldn't go anywhere. The sails drooped, the spinnaker flopped about, voluptuously caressing the forestay which it intended to embrace at the first opportunity, and our hearts sank. I fell to wetting my finger and holding it up in the air to find from which direction the wind was coming. This is a most useful and sensitive method of detecting wind and better than any telltale or other device on mast or rigging which will but perform circles in a very light air if the boat is rocking.

It is also useful to wet one's nostrils and, moving the head, discover which nostril becomes chilled, thus indicating the direction from which the air is moving. I learned this device not from a fellow sailor but from a professor of Physical Anthropology who assured me that our ancestors had wet noses (naked rhinaria was his phrase) and used them to detect wind directions and scents.

Well, thanks to the professor and our ancestors, I was able to detect tiny air currents and creep up on the competition. The wind, my nose and finger told me, was moving south and then a little west of south. It was nothing more than the faintest stir, hardly making itself felt on the spinnakers around me. But southwest of us, I saw *Porpoise III* and *Moonglow III* had dropped their spinnakers. So we dropped ours and sure enough the wind came in at last out of the southwest and off we went, blowing down the Strait, and ploughing our way over to the American side, which would favor us whatever the state of the tide.

We were alone when we got there except for *Suerte* which

was coming along well at perhaps two hundred yards behind us. All afternoon the wind held—really just a sailing breeze—out of the southwest, and by evening we were approaching the mouth of the Strait. Now *Jeunesse* had come over and risked all by going close to the American shore. We stood off a bit for the land was high there and the wind was likely to be blocked. We pulled ahead of *Jeunesse* by perhaps fifty yards but could not see our other competitor, *Rainbird,* who had, I believe, stayed over on the Canadian side—now drowned in the gold of the afternoon.

With sunset the wind went altogether, and *Jeunesse,* fighting a weaker tide than we, and perhaps getting a little cold air sliding down from the mountains, ghosted ahead of us. As for *Cu Na Mara,* she turned circle after circle in the middle of the Strait and at the mouth of it. Cape Flattery lay fine on my port bow, with Neah Bay abeam to port and Port San Jean over on the starboard. And when the sun went down the tide had swept us half a mile back into the bay and I looked at the chart and bemoaned the fact that there were one hundred and thirty fathoms of water under my keel and therefore anchoring was out of the question.

It is, of course, quite legitimate to anchor during a yacht race to prevent being swept backwards by the tide, and it is also legitimate to kedge, that is, to pull the boat forward by taking an anchor ahead of her, dropping it, and then pulling the boat up to her anchor. But the Strait of Juan de Fuca is deep and such tactics would not avail there. We sat waiting for the wind and the end of the long northern day.

When at last the sun had set and the mountains retreated into the fastness of the dark, a mild wind came up out of the northwest in little fits. We tried to sail by this, wondering where all the other yachts were. Their lights were not to be distinguished against the shore and the glum prospect was that they had managed to sneak out of the Strait and were now waltzing away for Hawaii while we drifted slowly back to Victoria.

The first watches of the voyage—scheduled watches—commenced at noon of the first day out while we were still in the Strait. Each man was to take one and a half hours on and then have a luxurious seven and a half hours off, though all were liable to call in case of a sail change.

This royal system could not be put into effect until we had taught Rob to sail. He was a quick learner and the only man I know whose first sail was a venture of two thousand miles. I discovered that Rob had some sterling qualities and among them was a spartan attitude in the face of disaster. In coming from Anacortes to Victoria before the start of the race, we had met very strong winds in the Rosario Strait and *Cu Na Mara* many times had been over on her ear with her lee rail awash. Rod had said nothing about this frightening situation but later asked Kevin what we did when the boat turned over. Kevin, astonished, explained that it was quite impossible to turn *Cu Na Mara* over. Her ballast and design would always bring her upright. This relieved Rob, who had expected that we would many times turn over in the middle of the ocean on our way to Maui.

Until Rob learned to sail, we would have to endure one and a half hours at the wheel and only six hours off. This hardship made us all eager teachers. Basically, we taught Rob to steer a compass course which he learned to do more quickly than anyone I have ever met. Once he could steer a compass course, he stood regular night watches and that system of pure luxury already referred to was put into effect on *Cu Na Mara*.

Most racing yachts have at least one man on deck at night besides the helmsman. I find that unnecessary and hard on the crew in that they lose sleep. The man at the helm is perfectly safe if he is fastened to the ship by a lifeline around his waist—something I insist on. If he needs help, he can blow a whistle or raise a shout and his relief will come up to his aid to trim a sail. If a sail change is needed, all hands can be called. Under the one-man-on-at-a-time system I find that the ship is safe, the men are safe, and everybody gets more rest—which makes the ship safer.

Cruising, I employ two-hour watches. But we were racing now, and an hour and a half was certainly enough for any man at the wheel. It would be better if a man was at the wheel for only half an hour at a time and then relieved. Such a system is used in big sloops and yawls with plenty of crew. It was a system we could not employ. Before the voyage was half over a crew of our size under such a system would be fatigued beyond caring whether the boat was moving along fast or not.

We were not clear of Cape Flattery until two in the morning after four hours of tacking in light winds. The tide took us out of the Strait. The wind was from the northwest outside the Cape though feather-light. It went around to the east a trifle and we ran before it, wing and wing with the Genoa out on the spinnaker pole. About three in the morning we changed to the light spinnaker which has a harp on it as an emblem. The harp is copied from that of Brian Boru (the name means Brian of the Cattle Tax, for so he raised his revenues) which may be viewed in any tavern in the world by ordering a bottle of Guinness.

About us, to the south, were the masthead lights of most of the fleet. When daylight came we could see one or two of the biggest boats west and south of us, and by noon we were fifteen miles south of Cape Flattery and could be said to have occupied the deep.

In twenty hours of sailing, however, we had covered scarcely ninety miles.

# *Chapter Fourteen*

WE HAD A GOOD shepherd for our racing fleet. The Royal Canadian Navy provided the escort vessel *Laymore,* Captain R. G. MacDonald commanding, to watch over us. Each noon—or at some other appointed hour, for the hour changed once or twice during the voyage—she went on the air and we heard the paternal voice of Alexander Forsyth on the radiotelephone making the roll call. "*African Star. African Star.* This is *Laymore.* Do you read me?" And *African Star* would call from the Bight of Benin or wherever she was, giving her position. And so it went the round of the fleet, each ship being called and reporting her position; or what she thought was her position, or what she wanted others to believe was her position. And these figures, the latitude and longitude, we on the *Cu Na Mara* took down carefully and plotted on an ocean pilot chart. And then we spent an hour mourning that so fine a boat as ours should be so far behind, or assuring each other that in the next day's run we would certainly make up the miles lost in the last twenty-four hours to our rivals.

All the way over, we never saw *Laymore*. If the United Nations should at any time be in need of a vessel which can stay out of sight, let me strongly recommend the Royal Canadian Navy as a place to look and the *Laymore* as the vessel to requisition. She was a Presence: firm, kindly, competent, and invisible. I asked her once whether she was really there, for by midpassage a sense of unreality was beginning to develop. She assured me that she was. But largely I took her on faith, and, trying to visualize her, I came up with as many variations as young Jim Hawkins had conjured of the "Sea Faring man with one leg" for whom he was to keep a weather eye open. Once during a dull wheel watch I convinced myself that she was a balloon drifting around in the stratosphere.

*Laymore* also broadcast a coded weather chart—a series of figures, painstakingly given and equally painstakingly copied down by Dan O'Brien who took over weather and chartwork for me, with the assistance of young Edwards.

From these figures a weather map of the greater part of the North Pacific could be constructed. This Dan did with infinite care every day and laid before me. And on this we looked about for that Ogre of the Deep, the North Pacific High. I think Dan found it once or twice breathing quietly out there to the west of us.

"I think it's west and north of us," he would say, and we'd look at each other. Then I would once again go through that formula for converting compass course to true course and look at the pilot chart and at the big mark I had made at 30 N. 138 W. where the trade winds were. Could we reach that place of safety before the monster reached out and sucked us up into his hot, still interior? My crew would gather around and we would assure each other that we would escape and find the winds and be free at last of the menace of that blind and mindless thing that roamed about the ocean seeking us.

I gave at these times what became almost a set piece on the subject of the trade winds. I described the sea changes and the cloud changes that heralded their approach and I told about the bosun bird with the long single tailfeather whom we would see and who was a sure sign that the trades were at hand. (Columbus sighted one of these birds, by the way, and took it as a sign that land was near, so you can quickly understand that anything seen at sea is a sign of something and sailors, being by nature optimists, usually take it to be something good.) My set piece about the trades having been given, all went about the ship's work with their minds composed and their determination strengthened.

A day or two out from Cape Flattery and I knew that I had, by greatest good fortune, got together an excellent crew. Kevin and Rob, of course, I knew. But George, Dan, and Bob Edwards were strangers, unknown quantities with unknown quirks and unknown weaknesses and strengths which would reveal themselves during the voyage and must be taken into account if we were to get the best out of the boat.

I had an international crew: two Americans, an Englishman, an Australian, and an Irishman (myself the latter). We represented what Winston Churchill once called "the English-Speaking Peoples." But although within that large compass there was room for many little national prides and rivalries, these never showed. Wind and salt water dissolved that whole mess. We melted into a thing called "crew"—a wonderful thing that sails ships in fair weather and in foul; that grumbles a bit and snarls a bit and laughs a bit and at the end of the voyage has woven between men a bond of regard and of affection which was well worth weaving.

My crew showed their special qualities early. Rob was assigned to the foredeck to help Kevin and George handle headsails and spinnakers. In the cockpit I had Dan and Bob. Halyards are the hardest things for amateurs to handle. "Here. Hold that," you say to a green hand, handing him the end of a halyard. He holds it and perhaps looks aloft. The halyard is to him just a rope that goes up there somewhere and disappears into the sky. But he has been told to hold the rope and he holds it.

Then comes another order: "Grab this," and he does what any sensible human being will do: he let's go the halyard and grabs the new offering, perhaps the leech of a sail or a winch handle. After all, he reasons, nothing much is liable to happen to a piece of rope hanging down from the top of a pole called a mast. It can't go anywhere. Alas, it can. The other end of that halyard is made of wire and it weighs more than the rope end. Let the rope end go and the wire end pulls it upward to the top of the mast and through the block, until it falls down the other side. And then there is nothing on which to raise the sail and someone has to go up to the top of the mast in a bosun's chair slung from another halyard and re-reeve the one that has come down.

The error does not belong entirely to green hands. I made it myself once, for I had done all my sailing on boats with all-rope halyards which were evenly weighted so you could let go the end without penalty. And then I crewed on a boat with a wire lead on the end of a jib halyard and I let the halyard go for a moment—and up it went to the masthead and down the other side while the rest of the crew regarded me with profound and unpitying contempt.

Rob made this error when we were a couple of days out. Given the end of the jib halyard to hold for a moment, he was given something else to hold and let go of the halyard. Up it went and tangled itself aloft following that law concerning lines already stated. The only solution was to go aloft on the main halyard and untangle the jib halyard. The bosun's chair was rigged and the crew hoisted me five feet off the deck. At that point the main halyard jammed, entangled by the jib at the masthead. I could go neither up nor down. I got out of the chair and at this point Bob Edwards revealed his sterling talents.

"I could climb up the shrouds, skipper," he said.

"Sure?" I asked.

"Yes," said Bob. "I've done it lots of times on my dad's boats." And sure enough, up he went, without benefit of bosun's chair, skinning up the mast and raising himself by the entwined halyards. He got the jib halyard down to us and then I went up in the chair to straighten out all aloft at leisure.

That was but the first of many trips aloft for me in that chair. But the great feat of seamanship was Bob's and although he thereafter showed a huge talent for losing things overboard, the voyage to the masthead more than made up for this.

Rob, in a day or two after this mishap, had become a most reliable foredeck man. He might not at all times know what was going on, but he did anything he was asked to do without flinching, whatever the weather. George became my expert on spinnaker nets, but I will get to that later. Dan, my other unknown quantity aboard, proved so remarkably good-humored, steady, sensible, and willing that I think I will miss him the rest of my sailing life. There are people who love disaster and when anything has gone awry, delight in the opinion that "nothing can be done about it." Dan was precisely the opposite. No matter what happened, he had a suggestion, and usually a good one, for remedying it. Yet he did not hold tenaciously to his proposal nor sulk if it was not adopted. A golden man to have on board was Dan O'Brien, and a staunch adversary of that Murphy who laid down Murphy's Law.

You know Murphy's Law of course. Its official title is "The Law of the Perversity of Inanimate Objects." Murphy's Law states, "Anything that can go wrong—will." Everyone is familiar with it. It will work, I am sure, at my funeral, for I confidently expect that whoever closes the lid of my coffin will catch my tie in it. It was, you will have perceived, Murphy's Law at work that caused the jib halyard not to go clear through the block at the top of the mast, but to wrap itself around the main halyard, so that I could not go aloft in the chair to untangle it.

We had many examples of the working of this malign principle as the race continued, and we came to blame Murphy himself for them, which was most unfair but eminently satisfying. Murphy became a Presence as the North Pacific High was a Presence and *Laymore* was also a Presence, though a benign one. We were even tempted at times not to mention Murphy's name lest we wake him up, and we began to take extraordinary precautions to forestall the workings of his law, which, as I have mentioned, we blamed on him, though he but recognized and defined it.

The first three days of the race we had variable winds, westerlies or north westerlies for the most part, interspersed with periods of flat calm. Whenever we got a wind we did well, for *Cu Na Mara* is a very fast boat. In light winds with the spinnaker—winds of say twelve knots—we were readily making eight knots, and when the wind dropped to the point where I had to wet my finger to find its direction, we could make half a knot or even a full knot, which was infinitely thrilling. Yacht racing is the only sport in which you can be overcome with joy at achieving a speed of half a mile an hour.

Three days out the westerly backed to southwest, heading us. It fell to a miserable dribble and had us heading ten degrees east of due south—a very poor course indeed. Still, I held on instead of tacking, for I had determined to get south as quickly as I could to reach the trades early and avoid the Monster out there to the east of us.

On the morning of July 4th, fog came with daylight. It was a strange fog: thick, silvery, blinding, and yet having with it a little wind. I am used to fogs developing in dead still air, but we were still able to sail, hearing here and there the sound of a steamer's foghorn, while unable to see past our bows. Just before noon the wind veered to the west again and came in stronger. We had been sailing close-hauled in the fog, but now were able to set the spinnaker again and hold the same due south course. The wind held during the remainder of the day, gradually increasing in force until at times we were showing ten knots on our speedometer, and charging southward first through fog and then through haze and finally, in the afternoon, in bright sunshine.

There was not much of a sea running. The waves were short and lumpy to the great joy of the spinnaker, which eyed the forestay with longing and tried time and again to envelope it, but was prevented by the spinnaker net. We were at this point, I believe, ahead of *Rainbird* and *Suerte,* but *Jeunesse* was sixteen miles to the west of us and headed more west than we. *Jeunesse* was brave and not afraid of the North Pacific High. Beyond her—several miles beyond—was the lovely *Porpoise III* with *Velaris* close on her heels. Both were going full tilt for Maui, undaunted by the basilisk which, if they sighted it, would turn them to stone.

For three days now, off and on, the spinnaker had been reaching its silken arms toward the forestay and had been baffled by the spinnaker net. But in the early hours of the morning of July 5th, in fact at two in the morning, during Rob's watch, the spinnaker got its chance. A swell passed under the boat, the spinnaker slipped over toward the forestay, and in the dark the spinnaker net must not have been watching, for the spinnaker wrapped itself around the forestay, the spinnaker net, the spinnaker staysail halyard, and as much of the spinnaker staysail as it could envelope.

"Spinnaker's wrapped," cried Rob when he realized what had happened. We tumbled out on deck and snapped on the spread lights to see what could be done. I am no veteran of this sort of thing, having a distrust of spinnakers as a sort of Oriental conspiracy which will one day bring down the whole Republic, but I have never seen such a wrap, even in photographs and when Kevin, who knew more about such things, saw it, he went several shades whiter. The whole sail was furled as tightly as an umbrella up the forestay, except for its top, which had formed into a lunatic bag of wind, flapping about in an idiotic manner at the masthead like a balloon on the end of a stick.

We started immediately to try to untangle it. We fell off the wind, we came up into the wind. We slacked the halyards. We hauled in on the halyards. We took down the pole and undid the guy and the sheets and we unraveled the spinnaker this way and that way. It was all to no avail. So avid was that jade of a sail to become one with the forestay that I began to think that the two could not be separated without burning them apart with a blowtorch, reducing the spinnaker to ashes.

Ah, the frustration of that wrapped spinnaker with its idiot balloon of wind up at the top of the mast flopping around in mockery! Eventually we tried wrapping the whole thing together like a huge snake and then uncoiling it from the forestay, and we twisted and twisted and twisted, but only succeeded in reducing the topmast balloon a little. We worked from two in the morning until four in the morning and had not the slightest success.

Then I dismissed the crew to continue their sleep, for I knew that that spinnaker could not be got down without my going to the top of the mast. Meanwhile *Jeunesse* and *Rainbird* and *Suerte* would be ploughing on toward Maui in this same brisk wind. *Porpoise III* and *Velaris* would certainly be galloping across horizon after horizon, and *Moonglow III,* the Cal 40, would be roaring southward to the trade winds. And *Cu Na Mara?* Why we crawled along across the deep with a balloon at our masthead, and a mainsail was all that we could get aloft.

I went to my bunk and dreamed of angels unwrapping the sail for me during the night. Then I dreamed of waking up and finding that the spinnaker had never really been wrapped at all. But then I woke up, about seven in the morning, there it was still, a silken coating for the forestay, and no sail at all. And there was the bag of wind wobbling away at the top.

"Give me a knife and rig the bosun's chair," I said, for I was going to cut the belly out of that bag of wind if it was the last thing I did on earth.

# *Chapter Fifteen*

TO GET A MAN to the masthead, the mainsail had to be lowered. The spinnaker, in wrapping, had made a clean sweep of all the other halyards. It had managed to envelope the jib halyard, the spinnaker staysail halyard, and the spare spinnaker halyard. The net itself did not go up on a halyard. It was an arrangement of elastic cord stretching between the mast and the forestay and sufficiently elastic not to interfere with the raising of the jib. But the elastic strands had broken and were all wrapped up in the spinnaker. The only halyard, then, on which to go aloft was the main. With the mainsail down and a medium sea running, the ship would be very unsteady and the job at the masthead would be that much more uncomfortable.

Up I went, armed with knife and pliers. All I had to do was to unshackle the spinnaker halyard from the top of the spinnaker, lower the halyard to the deck, and then untwist the spinnaker from the top, having first collapsed that balloon. The task was exhausting. The masthead swept through an arc of twenty feet, its rhythm broken by small arcs between the larger ones and jerks backward and forward. The first task was to remain in the bosun's chair and not get thrown either to the deck below, or overboard, which was of course the more preferable of the two. George, a little fair-haired mannikin at the wheel, tried to keep *Cu Na Mara* before the wind to lessen the side to side motion. But before I got the halyard unshackled and lowered to the deck I was almost without strength from the swinging about, my mouth was as dry as pumice, and my breath was coming in desperate gasps. I lowered the freed halyard and was brought down. Then Kevin and Rob and Dan and Bob tried to pull the spinnaker, no longer attached at the top, to the deck. The attempt was futile. It would not budge nor could it be unwrapped further.

Up I went to the top again. This time I could not cling to the mast for comfort but had to swing out to the forestay to try to unwrap the head of the spinnaker which had it in the embrace of a boa constrictor. Released from the halyard, the mocking bag of wind had collapsed and I felt that there was a considerable victory in that. But stretched between mast and forestay, swept from side to side with the rolling of the boat, I could not unwrap that spinnaker at the top, however hard I tried. I got a few turns undone and could do no more. On the ground, unwrapping would have been difficult because of the elasticity of the nylon sail. Up there, forty feet above the deck, swinging here and there, it was beyond my strength. The only thing to do was to cut the top off the spinnaker.

This in itself was no simple matter. I had to lean away from the comforting mast, grab the head of the spinnaker with one hand and work my knife with the other, so that I had no means of steadying myself in the swaying of the ship.

Nor could I tell, with the sail twisted, whether I was cutting through the shortest distance or not. I just plunged the knife in and cut away. It took great strength to get through the seams, but at last the head of the sail came away in my hand. I dropped it to the deck and it went overboard. Kevin fished it up before it sank, and in so doing, saved the sail—an act worthy of great praise.

You would think that now the sail would come down, but it still would not. We tried again from the deck, but could neither unwrap it nor pull it lower. I began to wish that I had a blow torch with me. Once more I went aloft and tried from the top. But the spinnaker was now too far from the mast, too far down the stay, for me to work on it. Plainly nothing could be done until I could get up the forestay itself, instead of up the mast.

So down again to the deck and this time, when I had rested a little, I went up the forestay, the chair being rigged to the stay on a shackle so it would ride up it. Up the forestay I went, a clumsy spider dangling from a swinging thread on the bow of the boat. Below, my poor crew suffered for me, tending the chair and the line rigged to it to prevent me from swinging completely around the stay in the rolling and pitching of the boat. Those not standing by the chair unwrapped the sail this way and that as I told them for that spinnaker wrap was not all in one direction but in two directions, running contrary to each other and each binding its opposite. I had to cut the spinnaker more to get it unraveled, but at last it came down. No squaresail, I assure you, could have given anything near the trouble provided by that spinnaker. At last all that remained was to unsnarl the jib halyard, the spare spinnaker halyard, and the remnants of the elastic from the net which encumbered the forestay like parasites clinging to a tree.

Finally all was done. The forestay was clear, the halyards were unsnarled, the mutilated spinnaker had been put in its bag, with instructions from me to bleed to death and we had raised the number two spinnaker, which was really a storm spinnaker. We had lost six hours of excellent wind and an estimated forty miles to our competitors. And then we fell into a high, a completely windless area, a part of that mindless and blind Thing, the North Pacific High, which had been seeking us. That night the wind dropped. By dawn we were all but motionless on water which betrayed not a single ripple from horizon to horizon. I had had the watch from two to three-thirty and had seen fine on the starboard bow a light and broad to port another light, both white.

I took them for the masthead lights of other yachts—*Rainbird* perhaps and some other. But they were not yachts. They were Russian whalers, rusty, a long way from home, and mounting harpoon guns on their bows. One came over to inspect us in the morning. We waved at each other across barriers of language, of culture, and of political belief. I raised Old Glory to identify ourselves as happy capitalists as they no doubt were happy communists. Away they sped, having looked us over in silence. Their bow wave and their wake made the only disturbance visible on the ocean.

Now those forty miles, perhaps more, lost during the spinnaker wrap really began to worry me. The high we were in, I reasoned, might be purely local, affecting only us. The other boats would be beyond it and sailing briskly for Maui while we baked on the molten sea.

George now began to display his special talent. He gathered together all the loose small stuff and elastic he could find on board, and, preempting the foredeck to his own use, settled down to make a new spinnaker net. He worked seriously and alone for the greater part of the day, and by mid-afternoon had made a splendid net, which with slight modifications, was to serve us staunchly for the rest of the voyage. Dan suggested that since we had eaten five days worth of supplies, it might be a good idea to check the stores and redistribute them to get a better ballast effect. I agreed that we ought to get all the weight possible in the middle of the ship and Dan busied himself with this task. Kevin took over the deck watches and I decided that in so profound a calm, I could profitably dive down to the rudder and see whether it was holding up and whether all was well with my centerboard, too.

So I clapped on a faceplate—denouncing my younger sons, Rory and Cormac, who had stripped the boat of snorkels for bathtub diving—and plumped overboard. Mercy but that water was cold. It shriveled my lungs to the size of walnuts in a moment and had me gasping for air for some seconds. And then my lungs adjusted, recommenced their function, and I dove below the surface to look at my enlarged and refastened rudder and my much strengthened centerboard.

All was well with the rudder. It looked efficient and strong, and though I gave it a good shaking, I could not move the gudgeon. Nor was there any antifouling paint cracked away from the gudgeon strap—a sure sign that it was holding well. The centerboard looked as wicked as a shark's fin. It was a sleek and cruel knife blade ploughing the water, and it could not be shaken either. So all was firmly in place below water. But around the propeller was a wreath of seaweed which we had perhaps dragged with us all the way from the Strait of Juan de Fuca, six hundred miles to the north. I cut it off with my knife and then looked about at the bland and empty blueness of the ocean. All about was infinity and infinity was the color of the sky. I floated then, in a thicker sky, solitary except for the strange sharklike shape of the boat underwater. Such thoughts make a man dizzy so I returned on board.

Here I want to say a word about smoking, which you can skip if you have already listened to too many words about smoking. I used to smoke until three years ago. I smoked perhaps a pack of cigarettes and three or four pipes of tobacco a day. I gave it up because I found myself ridiculously out of breath after only medium exertion. In my smoking days, when I went swimming I could stay only perhaps ten minutes in sixty-five-degree water and when I came out I shivered myself warm. Also I was getting very bald.

Some months after stopping smoking, I found an enormous improvement in my resistance to cold. I could stay swimming and diving in sixty-five-degree water without a wetsuit for half an hour or more. Exercise no longer left me breathless. And the two hairs on the top of my head have now increased to a hundred and perhaps more. All this, I think, resulted from the reopening of the capillary blood vessels which had been restricted, if not closed, by my daily intake of nicotine. It was not as hard to stop smoking as I had thought it would be. I was able to stop because I gave myself a positive rather than a negative reason for so doing. I asked myself if, by some miracle, I had received a new pair of lungs, would I smoke? The answer was no. So I pretended I had a new pair of lungs and it was quite easy to stop smoking to avoid coating them with nicotine.

I will add that everything of course started to taste more vividly. I found this a disadvantage, for I do not like the taste of many things and I preferred the old tastelessness of much food which I had to eat but didn't like. However, in every improvement there is bound to be a drawback. (Lettuce, closely considered, tastes like wet cobwebs.)

Well, we were in a high—a flat calm which persisted throughout the day and we spent our time, when the ship was taken care of, picking up the glass floats of Japanese fishermen which drifted gently by us. This was somewhat difficult to do with no wind, and therefore minimum steerage. Also we had the Genoa on the spinnaker pole which itself had a preventer on it, to stop it from slopping about. We spent an hour trying to pick up one particular glass float, getting the Genoa backed in the lightest of airs several times, but we were unable to get the float. In backing, the leech of the Genoa came against the shrouds several times, and that contact, unremarked at the time, cost us heavily later. We had, in all, two days in the high which we had gone south to avoid. We grieved deeply and wondered if others were also becalmed. But we feared that they were not. We were distressed by visions of *Jeunesse* and *Suerte* and *Rainbird* tearing along with full spinnakers while our spiritless mainsail flopped above us. We needed plenty of wind to make up the forty miles or so already lost, yet at times we had no steerage and at others we moved only enough to maintain some direction. In those two days of calm we covered only one hundred and ninety miles—a disastrous performance. And the midday roundup of boats showed that the others were pulling ahead, particularly *Jeunesse,* who was to the south and west of us and many miles away. *Jeunesse* we perceived had with enormous cunning and daring, avoided the high by sailing around its top edge. She had gambled on a straight line course to Maui while we, cowed by the threat of that questing beast, had gone south, sailed many more miles and fallen prey to that which we sought to avoid. We consoled ourselves with the thought that misfortune is unselective and the calm which had visited us following our spinnaker wrap might also visit others.

We did not say uncharitable things about the weatherman and his daily broadcasts. We reasoned that he was doing his best and was as much a victim of the weather as we. Also, in Victoria, enormous pains had been taken by Mr. Robert G. Brodie, chairman of the weather committee, to teach us all how to construct and read weather maps. We had been supplied with a generous quantity of blank weather charts and with kits with which to conjecture wind speeds. We had been given every facility possible to read the winds. The winds had proved unreadable, as unreadable as when Jason set out after the Golden Fleece. If we had no better luck than Jason, who were we to complain?

When we were altogether too dismayed and depressed about the lack of wind, I gave my set piece about the trade winds and the great speeds we would attain when we reached them. I pointed to the place on the chart where they were to be met (alas, it was six hundred miles away in a direct line) and recited a line or two of the Ancient Mariner to show that things could get a lot worse.

But it was nonetheless obvious after a week at sea, that we were never going to get to Maui in time for the victory dinner—nor, by the way, would the greater part of the fleet. We had made over six hundred miles in seven days (very poor going) and even on the rhumb line there were seventeen hundred miles to go. And we couldn't sail the rhumb line.

# Chapter Sixteen

DURING THAT PERIOD in the doldrums we got the light spinnaker repaired. Dan and George stuck it together with Ripstop and masking tape. After it was repaired, in an hour of very light wind, we raised the patched spinnaker and it drew well. Then we took it down again. The wind which had left us on the fifth returned in mid-afternoon of the seventh out of the southeast. The weather report spoke of a storm somewhere off Mexico and moving westward and we reasoned that the wind we were getting might be from this disturbance. Certainly we had no right to be experiencing a southeast, really south southeast, wind in our present position.

The choice was to fall off and head directly for Maui, or, reach for that place in the ocean where the trade winds were most likely to be met. I decided to follow the latter course and so we headed as close to south as we could, and our speed picked up from one to three and then to five and then to seven knots. By sundown we were making nine knots at times and it now seemed that we might be able to recover some of the distance lost during those two days of doldrums.

But Murphy, who had wrapped the spinnaker for us during Rob's watch and then given us two days of calm, was plotting other assaults.

Murphy picked Rob's watch again. We had taken down the spinnaker and replaced it with the Genoa for the wind had veered to the south and was heading us. To sail any meaningful course we must go close-hauled. Still we were boiling along handily when at three in the morning Rob yelled, "Genoa's split!" And so it had. It had split from about halfway up the leech or trailing edge all the way along a seam to the luff. Down it came and we had no sail to send up in its place.

"We'll sew it," said Dan. And we got out the needles and one of several bobbins of nylon thread I had aboard and started sewing. The split was about ten feet long and we were five hours repairing it. A patch had to be put in the sail at the leech where the split started. The sail had parted at this point through my neglect in picking up Japanese fishing globes. I had, at that time, let the edge touch and saw against the shrouds and that had chafed enough to permit the sail to split in the moderate wind.

We got the sail back on at eight in the morning, having lost perhaps another ten or fifteen miles to our opposition. The sail was up but an hour when it split along the same seam, starting again from the edge. Down it came, and we took off the reinforcing patch at the edge, which was of canvas. Dan cut a piece out of the sailbag, which was of dacron, and sewed this as a patch. The sailbag was brick red and the patch made a handsome effect on the white sail, like a cockade stuck in a hat. The dacron was also easier to sew and gave promise of lasting the rest of the voyage.

We looked the sail over carefully, found nothing else wrong, and sent it aloft again. But it had hardly been pulling half an hour before Kevin spotted three other small slits along another seam. A stitch in time saves not nine but nine thousand at sea and so the Genoa was hauled down once more and again we got out our needles and started sewing.

During the night, George and Kevin had helped with the sewing of that Genoa, Kevin with his eyes heavy with sleep. All told, I believe sixteen man-hours went into repairing that Genoa and the worst of it was that before setting out, I believed I had sent the Genoa to a sailmaker to have every seam gone over. Only later, on looking up the bill, did I discover that I had sent not the Genoa but the main. That error had come about because the mainsail had been put in the bag belonging to the Genoa. While it was a consolation to know that the main was not likely to split during the voyage, I would have been much wiser to have sent both sails to have their seams restitched before the race, although they were only a year old. It is folly to start a race of such length without this simple and inexpensive precaution. It was folly also to have spent so much of the doldrum period picking up Japanese fishing balls instead of looking over every inch of my sails. But after every mishap I am for a time the wisest and most skillful man on earth, and then I relapse to a more normal and comfortable state.

We were now eight days at sea. I had reckoned on a voyage of sixteen days at most. It appeared we would be at least twenty, and possibly twenty-one, days in reaching Maui due to the light winds at the start.

My forward water tank was low, and we were left with forty gallons of water—twenty-five in one tank and fifteen gallons in individual containers. To this could be added several gallons of canned fruit juices. Six men will use three gallons of water a day so I had a water supply for thirteen days, plus juices. That was enough to get me to Maui if nothing untoward happened—but supposing I dipped the spinnaker pole during some night of roaring wind and lost my mast? Then I might be not two weeks but three weeks before being picked up or making the islands under a jury rig.

I had to think in such terms and so passed the word that we would have to start rationing the water. A gallon a day would be enough for drinking, I thought, bulked out by fruit juices. All took the news cheerfully and in fact we never suffered any hardship from thirst, though our faces became salt-caked and our hands soiled. About every three days I allowed all hands to draw water to wash in so we were not seriously inconvenienced. We discovered, in fact, that the liquid in which our vegetables were canned was delicious to drink and we drank it with gusto.

There were, however, two shortages which were potentially more serious. The first was alcohol for the stove. The needle valve on one of the burners of the stove had developed a leak through not fitting properly; in addition some connection in the rear had worked loose. One day we poured half a gallon of alcohol into the stove reservoir and the next day discovered that it had all leaked out and the stove was empty. The same thing was done the following day and on later inspection the reservoir again proved empty. That the same mistake was made twice was the result of different people cooking each day. We had used in two days the alcohol supply for ten days, and from then on alcohol had to be rationed, only enough poured into the reservoir to cook one meal at a time.

The stove kept catching fire, as it had done since the first day I used it. We threw buckets of water over it. In fact, we kept a bucket of sea water in the cockpit for this purpose when cooking—that is until Bob lost the bucket overboard and in so doing revealed a remarkable characteristic. He had, he assured me, tied the bucket to a line with a perfectly sound bowline. He then put the bucket over the side to get some water and suddenly petrified us all by roaring at the top of his voice:

"GOD SAVE THE QUEEN!"

That was his way of announcing that the bowline had parted and the bucket had gone. This phrase, delivered fortissimo, was Bob's substitute for profanity. I will take profanity any day.

To the cry of "GOD SAVE THE QUEEN!" we discovered that Bob had thrown half our flatware overboard with the dishwater.

"GOD SAVE THE QUEEN!" likewise announced the loss of a shirt and a towel.

But Bob, for all this, was a good seaman and a staunch hand and having gone up the halyards to unsnarl a tangle for me at the start of the voyage, I was willing to forgive him many peccadilloes. I think he had a "thing" about throwing stuff overboard. At the start of the race he came storming up from below and threw overboard a carton of cigarettes, vowing that he would not be so weak-minded as to continue to smoke throughout the voyage. Then he cadged a cigarette or two from Dan who was by no means given to such Draconian measures.

The other shortage that threatened us was one of matches. Smokers are very careless about matches and leave them about here and there. Matches left in the cockpit overnight are soaking wet by the following morning, and checking over my supply after the first week at sea, I found we had but seven boxes left. So matches had to be rationed, and the sticks of wooden matches were no longer to be thrown overboard. They were to be put back in the match box and if a second burner on the stove was to be lit, it was to be lit with a used match.

What I was guarding against there in the conservation of water, and of alcohol, and of matches was wastage. It is a wastage of time in not repairing something immediately, in not making the best use of calms to be ready for storms. And it is wastage of material bringing to the sea those habits of plenty which belong solely to the land.

Our troubles with the Genoa and with the spinnaker, coupled with the two days of no wind or light wind, had caused us to drop behind all the boats in our class. My noon sight on July 9th showed we were in latitude 38 north and longitude 134 west. We needed to get four hundred miles further south and two hundred and forty miles further west to get to the trades. I could not lay the course direct to that glorious spot where I would meet the trades for the wind was from the southwest and thus right in our eyes. I had to head as close to south as I could, and so set the course. The wind was light and gave us at best only six knots and our daily run was disappointing—ninety miles on the eighth of July, one hundred miles on the ninth, one hundred miles on the tenth. I began to dread the noon sight which was of the greatest importance now since we were running south.

I started taking it half an hour before the meridian was reached and groaned as the sextant reading showed us still well to the north. Looking upward it certainly seemed that the sun was almost directly overhead and the sextant should then read ninety degrees. Instead it read in the mid-seventies and in black moments I wondered whether it had not been damaged.

The ninth of July was a bitter day. The best course we could make was due south magnetic which was somewhat east of south true, so that in making our southing we were actually sailing away from Hawaii. And if I tacked I would be sailing away from those longed-for trade winds. The wind went lighter and lighter and headed us as it did so. By mid-afternoon, the best course that could be steered was southeast. We tacked to southwest and almost immediately the wind died to nothing. All day long our highest speed was three knots and at times it fell to zero. Had we indeed, then, in spite of all our care, fallen again into that North Pacific High? Was it possible that that ogre had silently stolen eastward as we tried to slip south past him? And what of our competitors? Was *Jeunesse* bowling along to the west of us—far to the west of us—in a brisk breeze, and *Rainbird* and *Suerte* also?

Devoid of comfort, I called *Laymore*—kindly, protective, benign *Laymore*. I assured *Laymore* that I did not want to know her position. I assured *Laymore* that I did not want to know anything about her other than to inquire whether, wherever she was, she had any wind, for it seemed to me that the last of the wind had been drained off from the earth.

*Laymore* replied consolingly that in the mysterious regions in which she was, she had two knots of wind. Then came *Oriole,* eighty-three-foot *Oriole,* somewhere south and east of us, saying that where they were they were about to become airborne, and if we were in need they would send us a CARE package.

My crew, who, with the notable exception of George, rarely wrote anything at all in the Racing Log, relieved their feelings by now noting the state of the wind in the logbook, so that there could be a written record of the manner in which it had served us. George's entry was as follows: "Came on watch with a light wind S.W. making 2½ knots but up to 4½ for short periods. 7:20. Wind veering. Steered 170 then progressively lower. Called skipper 7:30. Tacked. Then wind died. Tacked, tacked again and headed for catspaw sighted by Dan 8:15. Having found wind and sailed well clear of hole, tacked again and resumed course. Hoisted racing burgee." (It was a splendid burgee, given to all the competing yachts and depicting symbolically the track of the boats from Victoria to Maui.)

My own entry was; "No wind over 3 knots." Rob wrote; "Wind disappointing." Kevin, disgusted, just signed his name in the logbook but with no comment. We didn't get anything you could call a wind in a Christian country until the eleventh and on that day made one hundred and thirty-five miles.

George spent his spare time making a new spinnaker net and produced a dilly. And on July 12th, when we should have been almost able to smell the flowers on the Hawaiian islands, the wind picked up. It came out of the southwest, but veered west by four A.M. and by dawn had gone around to the north. During the dawn watch I smelled something promising in the air, a combination of warmth and of moisture, that suggested that the trades were not far off. By six in the morning, after three days with the Genoa, we ventured to set a spinnaker at last and we got up the light chute which had been stuck together and then sewed together by Dan and George. Now we could head directly for our rendezvous with the trades which I believed were hardly a day's sail away.

How wonderful it was to have a spinnaker flying again—wonderful in the increase in speed, in the liveliness of the boat. But a little more troublesome on the helm for I soon found that if *Cu Na Mara* was allowed to come higher than 210 magnetic, she would broach. The light spinnaker drew so well, all stitched as it was, that I determined to take it down, put up the storm spinnaker and do a little more work on the light one. We changed and with the heavy chute up charged along at seven to eight knots, with a sea that was beginning to run from the starboard quarter so that at times we could surf on it.

*Jeunesse* and *Rainbird* and *Suerte,* according to their radio reports, were far to the west of us. But now we were in *Cu Na Mara*'s weather and romping with glee across the ocean. The sun was out strong and hot and the sea sparkled and crested white against a dazzling blue around us. The sloop leaned her lovely white shoulder into the ocean and slipped forward and she kept up her canter hour on hour and mile after mile.

By dawn of July 13th, we had had our first twenty-four hours of real racing with the spinnaker pulling every minute. The sea had gone round to the starboard quarter—a sure sign of the approach of the trades—and on those following seas *Cu Na Mara* surfed sometimes a hundred or two hundred yards at a time. Surfing, the needle of the speedometer went over to the stop at ten knots, so she was traveling faster than that, and she left a lovely, flat creamy wake behind her, stretching away like a ribbon. An hour after sunrise I sighted the first bosun bird, a little white dovelike thing with a ridiculously long tailfeather, fluttering futilely against the wind. And so we sped on, happy with the whole world, exulting in the swift beauty of our yacht and the golden sun and azure sea.

I took my noon sight, worked it out and Dan, who was at the wheel, called, "How many miles, Skipper?"

"Two hundred and twenty, noon to noon," I said. The silence that followed was more eloquent than a cheer.

# *Chapter Seventeen*

YOU WILL PERCEIVE that for twenty-four hours we had outwitted Murphy of the infamous law, but we had not forgotten him. Indeed, making such splendid progress we had him strongly in mind and to thwart his plans, that afternoon we took down the spinnaker and raised the Genoa. I looked over the spinnaker halyard carefully. It seemed to me that there was some chafing of the splice in the end, so I cut out the end and respliced it. Then we sent the spinnaker aloft once more, comforting ourselves with the thought that we had forestalled Murphy's plans.

At ten in the evening of the previous day the wind had been out of the north northwest. By five in the morning of July 14th it had veered to northeast and we were at last in the trades. The bosun bird had not lied and we could look now for a steady wind, increasing in strength as we went south and blowing directly toward the Hawaiian Islands.

Concurrent with the arrival of the trades, Murphy struck

again. George was at the wheel and called "All hands! All hands! Spinnaker halyard's parted."

Out we tumbled, wondering how the halyard could have parted when I had just respliced the end. But it was not the halyard that had gone at all. The block at the masthead through which the halyard passed had pulled apart. We raised the spinnaker on the jib halyard and were underway once more in twenty-five minutes. After breakfast I went to the masthead and installed a new block for the spinnaker and rerove the halyard. The seas were quiet and the wind moderate (since we were just entering the trade wind belt) so that task was not difficult. In half an hour all was done. The wind continued light and we sent up the light spinnaker. But a hole soon appeared in it where it had been stuck together at the head so down it came and up went the storm spinnaker while Dan and George repaired the hole.

We had had three hundred yards of nylon thread aboard at the start of the race. Between sewing the Genoa three times and the spinnaker twice we had used up all of it except a few feet which were put aside for emergency. I had, however, a few hundred yards of good sail twine and a supply of sail needles so I was not worried on this score. (For work on spinnakers and other light sails, regular sewing needles are superior to sail needles, but it is a good idea to carry both kinds. With the regular needles you need a thimble, and for the sail needles a sailmaker's palm and a pair of pliers.)

That evening we had another go-around with Murphy, whose favorite sail was the spinnaker. It had become a custom to play a few hands of bridge each evening during the second dogwatch from six to eight. Since nobody really knew how to play the game, no conventions were observed and bidding often developed into a lunatic feud between partners. When it was not a feud between partners, it was a feud between opposites and it was extremely difficult to persuade Rob that you had won nothing by winning the bid. He once bid his hand up to five hearts on the premise that since he had four hearts in his hand, there must be at least one in his partner's making five all told. He tended to regard any bid higher than his as a personal affront. (I think another reason for his monstrous bidding was that he didn't like to be dummy.)

Anyway, in the midst of our play, Dan shouted that the spinnaker, the light one, was splitting again. We flung the cards on the table and piled on deck and got it down fast. Then we sent up the storm spinnaker in its place. But the storm spinnaker had been wrongly packed and went up twisted. The wind which had been light all day had increased somewhat and the twisted spinnaker was jerking away at the mast, shaking it vigorously. George was on the guy and started to pay off the line to spill the wind from the sail. But the sail, untwisting further at that moment, filled suddenly and pulled the line, smoking, through George's hands. He got a rope burn so severe that he could do nothing but tuck his hands under his arms in agony.

Meanwhile the spinnaker, untwisted, was flying off the end of the mast like a kite. It was attached by its halyard and by the sheet, but the halyard had been started in the confusion so that the head of the sail was twenty feet from the masthead. It was an impressive sight, but unfortunately at such times one cannot use a camera. The spinnaker, billowing and jerking to leeward, had enormous leverage and was jerking the mast so heavily that the whole boat shook. I feared the mast could collapse at any moment. The only solution was to wind the spinnaker back aboard by the sheet. We could have let the halyard go entirely, but that would have meant another trip to the masthead for me to re-reeve it and I had had enough of such trips. We got the spinnaker back on board and found a small tear in the foot. This I sewed up, cursing Murphy, and the spinnaker went back up an hour later. George's hand, however, was so painful that he was excused from standing his wheel watch that night. Our day's run, when I took the noon sight on the morrow, was only a hundred miles. Murphy was winning in his contest. We had reached the trades at last only to find them light. During the night, in fact, we drifted rather than sailed, with scarcely enough air to keep the spinnaker full.

*Jeunesse,* seemingly with much more wind and sailing a shorter course, was now almost three hundred miles ahead of us—two full days of sailing. Beautifully handled, she had managed to avoid the high which had trapped us twice so far. There was little hope of catching her. According to her daily radioed position, she had been able to hold a course direct for Maui. *Rainbird* was not much closer and even *Suerte,* to whom we had to cede time, was well ahead of us. Light winds, head winds, sail drills, and calms had cost us very heavily and now that we had reached the trades, even they were disappointing. Hoping to find some good news to cheer the crew, I tried to get a positive fix with three stars that night. But the entire horizon was obscured by cloud, even at twilight. "Tomorrow the wind will be stronger," I promised. "We will be deeper in the trades. We'll get some good surfing and pick up some of that lost mileage."

But it was quite obvious that the winds which were strong for us would also be strong for *Jeunesse* and *Rainbird* and *Suerte,* let alone *Porpoise III,* four hundred miles ahead of us, *Velaris,* and the rest. But I did know that when it came to surfing I could outperform *Rainbird* and maybe *Suerte* and even *Jeunesse,* for *Cu Na Mara* will surf on a ripple.

So we comforted ourselves with crumbs. (Such crumbs have brought men through all the long hazards of history and are not to be disdained.) Our position in our own class was bad. But in respect to the other and bigger boats it was not so depressing. *Mary Bower,* racing in Class II, was close by and we were boat for boat ahead of *Oriole* and *Potlatch* and *Cubara,* all of whom were much bigger than we. But what magic had they aboard *Jeunesse* that they were able to do so well? Was there a Finn in her crew—for the Finns are able to control the winds, as is well known. Kevin said that part of the magic was that they had better spinnaker gear, but I think there was something Finnish about them, and certainly no man can prevail against the black arts.

The wind did pick up on the following day, as I had prophesied, and moved around more to the east. We had a day's run of a hundred and thirty miles and were grateful for that extra thirty miles, though it was not a creditable racing performance. With the wind light we used, of course, the light spinnaker and holes kept appearing in it for it was only stuck together and loosely basted. Eventually we took it down and Dan and I resewed the whole thing with small stitching, using up every inch of nylon thread left on board. But thereafter it did not split and it set splendidly.

Now the wind kept going more and more to the east, under the influence, I believe, of that Mexican storm of which we had received some warning. At last it went so far to the east that on the starboard tack we were sailing a little north of west, away from the islands. We jibed when Murphy was not looking and managed to flop across the wind in a few seconds without anything getting fouled.

Maui was now nine hundred miles away. We had been fifteen days at sea and were in the rearguard of the race, behind everybody in our class. We were also very tired. We got plenty of sleep to be sure, we had good food, even though it was getting monotonous. But a heavy fatigue was settling on us, the result of concentrating for so long on one objective—and failing to achieve it. Nobody was downhearted. Nobody grumbled. But I found my temper getting short and I had to watch that I did not get irritated over trifles. I very nearly had a run-in with Dan who was so good a seaman and so goodnatured that I am almost ashamed to mention it. I had decided to try to get a fix using Antares and Vega. Vega I brought down readily and handed the sextant to Dan to read for me in the light of the cabin, for when you are taking star sights it is necessary not to destroy your night sight by going into a bright light until all the sights are taken. Dan handed me back the sextant and I got an altitude of Antares, but it was uncertain because there were many clouds on the horizon under the star. This irritated me because a fix using two stars would have been very useful at that stage, and now my fix would be doubtful. But what irritated me more was Dan's announcement that the star I had taken first could not possibly be Vega, for the altitude was too much by twenty degrees. I told him that it was Vega and that I knew Vega as well as I knew the lamp post outside my front door. He said there must be a mistake and I went down into the cabin to take the Star Identification Chart from him and demonstrate to him beyond all possibility of doubt that the star was indeed Vega and that he was entirely wrong.

"Work the sight yourself then," said Dan.

So I worked it and Dan was right—the altitude was far too much. I said nothing but went out of the cabin to cool off. And it was only next day that the true explanation occurred to me. In handing the sextant down to Dan, the clamp had loosened and the altitude he had read off the arc was not the altitude I had obtained from Vega. This was fatigue at work—nerves rubbed a little raw and sense of proportion lost.

To compensate for our many frustrations we now started to pick up a little speed. By the sixteenth we had narrowed the gap on *Rainbird* by a hundred miles and we were, according to the radioed positions, ahead of *Suerte* who had been well ahead of us. We could only reason that they had both fallen into windless areas for we ourselves had not had a remarkable run in the past twenty-four hours. Whatever the explanation, there was a chance now of getting second place in our class if we could just manage to keep going and escape the wiles of Murphy.

Murphy, however, was not to be so easily eluded. We had had the spinnaker up for thirty hours and we had made one twenty-four hour run of one hundred and fifty miles, which was close to respectable, when at midnight, on George's watch, the swivel on the spinnaker parted and down came the sail. (Have you noticed, by the way, that these things always happened at night? Remember the full version of Murphy's Law: Anything that can go wrong, will go wrong, and always at the worst possible time!)

We had been flying the spinnaker on the jib halyard which has a wire tail. During the squalls the spinnaker would fill suddenly and give a tremendous jerk at the masthead and I think that it was this jerking which had pulled the swivel apart, for the wire tail of the halyard would not stretch to provide a spring. We sent up the Genoa and ran wing and wing until the following morning when young Bob volunteered (I being tired of the trip) to go to the masthead and bring down the halyard. On deck we found that flying a spinnaker from a jib halyard with a wire tail is not a very good idea. There were two pieces of aluminum forward of the mast through which this halyard led. They had chafed on the halyard so badly that the stainless steel six-strand wire was almost worn in two. I had to cut off the end and make a new eye in it with cable clips so it could be used again.

Everybody at this point was beginning to hate the spinnaker. The very mention of the sail produced a sort of flinching, but we sent it up again on its own halyard and held on, waiting for it to split or come down again or knock us over on our ears in the ocean.

Ahead of us, standing guard around the Hawaiian Islands, we knew, were whole regiments of squalls. You could see them coming—dark cloud masses with a thicket of rain below them, descending on the ship. In the daytime, seeing a squall build up and approach, it was possible to square off and run before the squall at hull speed. But at night these squalls were fearful creatures, heard rather than seen, for the sound of the rain and the wind roared in the blackness of the ocean. Then the helmsman had to brace himself and be ready to square off as soon as the squall hit. *Cu Na Mara* would boil along in a smother of foam which though it could not be seen in the dark could be heard. She moved so fast she dug herself a hole in the water and if the wave action pushed her around so that the weight of the squall struck abeam, then she tried her best to broach or get broadside to the wind and every ounce of strength and of prayer was needed at the wheel to hold her head off. Broaching in such a squall, she would be knocked down and a knockdown in the dark of the night is a horrifying experience.

Coming now, as we approached the islands, into its defense works of squalls, we had all of us great wrestling matches with wind and waves, with rain and dark. Something else was added to this. On really dark nights we suffered a kind of vertigo unconnected with seasickness and fearful to endure. I first experienced it on a black night in which squall followed squall within minutes of each other. All there was before me in the blackness and confusion, was the glowing pink hemisphere of the binnacle. Nothing else could be seen but this pink mound with the compass card swinging below it. *Cu Na Mara* rolled, writhed, twisted, and plunged in the blackness as squall after squall overtook her. To keep the ship on course, I had to watch the compass closely; to head her off the wind, I had to watch the compass to see that I did not swing too far off or let her round up too much. In short, all I had with which to orient myself was that swinging card in its horrid pink bubble. As the ship continued to plunge and writhe below me, I lost my orientation and began to feel that I was not on a ship at all, nor on anything solid, but that I was free-falling through space, turning over and over, rolling to one side and then to another, without any control, and before me a pink globe also was tumbling through the void of space, maintaining an exact distance ahead. The sensation was exactly the same as that experienced in those terrible dreams of falling which are common to us all. But this was a "falling dream" from which it was not possible to wake up and find all was well. I felt myself falling through thousands of miles until, unable to endure it further, I called to the watch below to turn on my navigation lights. And when they were on, the nightmare went for I had something to relate to other than the swinging compass in its pink hemisphere. It was terrible while it lasted though, and I was clinging to the wheel in something close to panic, not to steer the ship but to have something to hold to in that free fall through nothingness.

Deep in the squall zone, determined to catch up to *Rainbird* and *Jeunesse,* we carried our spinnaker in winds which I believe were often of forty knots. *Cu Na Mara* traveled so fast that three distinct stern waves flowed out from behind her and in addition she threw quarter-waves off the extreme corner of her transom which looked like those of a powerboat. I have never seen so small a boat move so fast under sail; in the heavier gusts she settled so deep in the water that it seemed her huge bow-wave would come clear over her deck. You could feel her being driven deep into the water by the speed at which she was traveling and I began to calculate the hull pressure and hope that fiberglass was as strong as I believed it to be.

*Cu Na Mara* was in fact traveling at a speed fifty percent greater than her hull speed (that is the theoretical speed at which the hull can travel through the water without starting to founder). Her wake, even in the angry ocean strewn with whitecaps, stretched out behind her like that of a liner. We were really surfing, adding miles per day to the distance actually sailed. On noon of July 19th, we had covered one hundred and ninety-five miles in twenty-four hours and this despite the fact that Murphy got at the spinnaker block again (at midnight of course) and pulled it apart, so that we had to travel for eight hours on the winged-out Genoa.

The morning of the following day, the twentieth, broke wet and stormy. The air was heavy with moisture and there was heavy rain in the squalls. The seas were big, dark, and cresting. I had once more to go to the masthead to install a new block for the spinnaker halyard, this being, I think, the sixth ascent of the voyage. Conditions were very bad at the masthead, due to the exaggerated motion aloft and when I got the block installed I found, to my disgust, that I had neglected to tie the end of the halyard to my bosun's chair. Again, I went back down to the deck for the halyard and then aloft once more, so that by the time it was rigged,

I was bruised about the arms and chest from being battered against the masthead and the shrouds.

The wind had got worse while I was aloft, but worse or not, I determined to get the spinnaker up as soon as possible. Kevin suggested that we couldn't carry it in the rising wind and I told him to get it up anyway. The spinnaker went up twisted. A squall caught it and in an instant we were knocked down on the water, the mast vibrating like a fishing pole. We got it down, untwisted it, and I ordered it up again. As soon as it was up full it took control of the ship and put her once more flat in the water. Down it came again only to go up again. When we were knocked down for the third time, I conceded that we should not be flying the spinnaker.

"Get the Genoa up then," I said. Up went the Genoa. *Cu Na Mara* darted off like a stag and the Genoa split from clew to luff.

I looked at the twelve-foot rip in the Genoa, at the furious sea and wind which prevented me flying a spinnaker and recalled that we had almost no nylon thread left on board with which to repair the sail.

"What next?" I demanded.

At that moment a couple of destroyers came up over the horizon and one of them started firing at us.

# Chapter Eighteen

THE DESTROYERS, *Isbell* and *Waddell*, came up on us from northeast, traveling fast. We had heard beforehand several rumbles of what appeared to be thunder, for the day was stormy with great curtains of clouds hanging about the skies and squalls here and there heavy enough to obliterate the horizon. When first seen, the destroyers looked like two enormous ketches making a passage from California to Hawaii. Dan got the glasses on them and for a while could not make them out, but soon they were hull up over the horizon and close enough for us to see with the naked eye that they were destroyers.

I was at the wheel, and we were running downwind with the main only. The boom was held with a preventer so the work at the wheel was not particularly bad. Dan and George were below mending that split Genoa. Suddenly I noticed a flickering light from the aftermast of the destroyers and thought she was signaling us, but the flashes were far too fast for me to read any message.

A moment later Kevin, who was atop the cabin, cried out, "Dad! They're firing!" I saw the splash of a shell back astern of us. Two more shells splashed immediately after, each nearer, and in rapid succession, before I reacted. I could not believe that we were in any danger for the destroyers were no more than five miles away and therefore I assumed that they could very easily see us.

However, when another shell fell very much closer, and in our wake—they had all been in line with our course—I told Kevin to get on the radiotelephone on 2182, the international watch frequency, call the ships and tell them that we were in their line of fire. Kevin did this but could get no acknowledgment from the destroyers. I told him to try to contact our Canadian escort, *Laymore,* and have *Laymore* contact the destroyers. Actually we raised *Oriole,* who relayed our message to *Laymore* who called Honolulu. A couple more rounds had meanwhile come hurtling through the air. At the wheel, I could not look behind to see the fall of shot for fear of gybing the ship.

"Next one will hit us," said Dan.

The next one plopped into the water about five hundred yards astern. We waited for the end, and then the firing ceased. The two destroyers remained for a while, one closing in on the other as if for consultation. Then they took off for Hawaii at high speed, like a couple of kids who had flung a baseball through somebody's window and didn't want to stay around to be caught.

I was a bit peeved. I figured that the destroyers might at least have come over to see whether any damage had been done to us. The course on which they departed would take them deeper into the racing fleet. We called *Oriole* again to warn the destroyers through naval headquarters in Honolulu not to resume firing as they would be firing into the middle of a yacht race. We figured about eight rounds had been fired at a constant range but on a bearing which was closing on us. Of course, there was no suggestion at all in our minds, then or later, that we were being used as a target. Yet it was remarkable that, at a distance of five miles, we could not be seen either visually or by radar.

When the firing was over we forgot about it because we had some very pressing problems to attend to. The first of these was the repair of the Genoa. We had run out of thread, but I had that sail twine and some heavy needles. We broke these out and started sewing. The sail needles had to be pushed through the dacron with a pair of pliers which made the work slow. We used fairly big stitches and meanwhile put up the little green and white spinnaker staysail to get as much push as we could, for we were still racing. We now had no hope at all of coming in first in our class or of placing in the overall race.

*Jeunesse,* beautifully handled by Skipper Cote, was two days ahead of us. Murphy was not aboard her, and her skipper had outguessed that ogre of whom we had stood in such fear—the North Pacific High. He had sailed west and north of it. We, going south and more to the east, had fallen into it. So *Jeunesse* would win first in our class and looked as if she might be second overall. Our slim hope lay in taking second in our class. To do that we had to sew fast and find a way of exorcising Murphy. Murphy was still aboard. Half an hour after the destroyers had ceased firing the clew of the spinnaker staysail tore out. It didn't tear along the seam. It tore clean across the seams and how that happened not even the sailmaker to whom I showed it later could guess. It cost thirty-five dollars to restitch it ashore.

We were left then with just a mainsail for the wind was so gusty that we couldn't raise the spinnaker. I think the general force of the wind was about twenty-five knots and the squalls were fifteen knots more. That is a guess, but the ocean was covered with patches of foam, the crests on the waves were yards long, and thunderclouds mounted about us on every side like canyon walls. In mid-afternoon we saw a tremendous spectacle. A huge mass of cloud loomed like a cliff on the starboard bow. There were layers and layers of this cloud, reaching upward into the heavens, light in parts and deep purple in others. The sensation of vertical ascent was so strong that we felt dizzy looking at it. Tier upon tier of cloud soared skyward and the base was as solid on the ocean as a pillar of ebony.

While we watched, rain started to fall from the topmost tier of this cloud. It seemed to arch out, like a waterfall in the sky and cascade downward, glittering in the wan sunlight to fall into the dark base on which the whole structure was erected. There was a cataract of a thousand feet or more in the sky, the water plunging from one ledge of cloud down into another far below, there to be lost. It was a scene from some wild and fantastic land, and it ended with the cloud mass turning into one solid curtain of rain that seethed into the ocean and passed scarcely half a mile to starboard of us.

Three hours were spent sewing up the split in the Genoa. We all sewed on it and finally we got it up an hour before sunset, then we turned on the radio to see if we could, despite the atmospherics, get Honolulu. To our surprise, the first item on the news was the story of the two destroyers firing on us and we discovered we were famous.

Each successive broadcast devoted more and more time to the accident, and when, at six in the evening, we tuned into *Laymore* for the weather broadcast, she asked us to give her, at noon on the following day, the full and official story, including time of the firing, our position, type of ammunition used, range of the destroyer involved, bearing and so on. All this was easy enough to supply and Rear Admiral F. E. Bakutis, Commandant Fourteenth Naval District, acknowledged the error and apologized through the press. When I got back to California I wrote Admiral Bakutis and he replied saying that *Cu Na Mara* could not be seen visually or by radar and was not spotted until immediately after *Isbell* ceased firing.

It was very lucky for us that *Isbell* did cease firing when she did, for judging from the previous fall of shot, the next round would have come very near us or perhaps have hit us. The Admiral apologized once again and concluded with the suggestion that radar reflectors be carried in rigging or at the masthead to help other ships to see a yacht. This of course is common practice among yachtsmen in fog or at nighttime. What is new is that it would appear necessary to carry a radar reflector day and night, in fog or clear weather, when sailing near shipping. My aluminum mast with stainless steel shrouds and stays going to the top, had not been seen on the radar screen of either the *Waddell* or the *Isbell*. Come to think of it, the two freighters who had collided that night off California when I had turned back hadn't seen each other either, though both had radar.

Radar is, at best, only an aid; yet I think in making another ocean crossing, I would try to keep a radar reflector aloft day and night.

# *Chapter Nineteen*

We were now only three hundred miles from Maui and were concentrating on snatching second place in our class from *Rainbird*. It is surprising how relative a matter distance is. Had we been starting a race of three hundred miles, we would think we had a long, hard haul before us. But finishing a race of over two thousand, that three hundred miles seemed like nothing. The trades were now very heavy, twenty-five knots I would judge. The seas were streaked with foam and there were many squalls during which the course had to be abandoned and the ship run off before them. There was, for a while, bright sun, so sights could be taken and our position exactly located. A course of 225 true would bring us to Maui right on the nose, and it seemed that we were now slightly ahead of *Rainbird* and well ahead of *Suerte* in the distance to be covered to Maui. We were also ahead or abreast of many bigger boats racing in other classes, according to their broadcast positions.

However, at noon on the nineteenth of July, a marvelous revision of positions came over the air from the other boats, who either had had fantastic runs during the last twenty-four hours, or had, in chorus, discovered astonishing errors in their navigation. One vessel altered her position by three hundred and forty miles, another by two hundred and thirty-five, and another by three hundred and twenty—splendid runs, surpassing those of the fastest clippers. On that same day, pressing *Cu Na Mara* as fast as we might, the best we could achieve was one hundred and sixty miles, almost exactly matching *Rainbird*'s run for that day.

Vessels which had been behind us were now well ahead, having developed overnight either the speed of *Cutty Sark* or more competence in navigation. The radio announced that *Porpoise III,* whose position was always correctly given, had already crossed the line—first to finish and first in her class—and she was followed by *Velaris* and by *Moonglow.* Then we heard that *Jeunesse* was in, so she had won our class. But there was still *Rainbird* to compete against and still a chance of making a showing overall on corrected time.

We tried the spinnaker again, not once but several times, because we were really determined to do our best to beat *Rainbird.* We would get it up for perhaps two or three minutes and then would come one of those squalls, streaking the ocean with straight lines of foam, and *Cu Na Mara* would hover on the very edge of control. Down would come the spinnaker, for we couldn't afford to lose our mast or rigging at this point. Then up again and down again.

Eventually I decided that it was a waste of time trying to fly a spinnaker on *Cu Na Mara* in winds of over thirty knots. We stuck to the poled-out Genoa and the unreefed main, making a steady six and a half knots, but with control at all times. By noon of July 20th we were a hundred and sixty miles from the big luau and prize presentation which was to be given that evening. We couldn't make it so we had a plain, healthy meal of beans, peas, and spam instead. To relieve the nerves of my crew I told them that we would not raise the spinnaker again, and that we would be in plain sight of Maui by four in the afternoon of the following day. I don't think they believed me on either count.

That night, during my watch, a steamer almost ran us down. She came up on the starboard on a collision course and although I floodlit my sails by turning on my spreader lights, the steamer made no course alteration. She ploughed relentlessly on, plainly without any deck watch at all, for my illuminated mainsail certainly made a huge splash of white light in the ocean.

When it seemed that she would certainly run us over I called all hands and got the preventer off the mainsail, dropped the spinnaker pole, and gybed the ship. This is no easy operation in a twenty-mile-an-hour wind and a vigorous running sea. The steamer passed within two hundred yards of me, still on the same course, still without having seen me. So much for the lookout of the merchant marine. You will recall that at the start of my voyage, two steamers equipped with radar had rammed each other within five miles of my position in a fog.

Without consulting my sextant I knew at this point that we were close to the islands for the wind had gone around to south of east and there were flocks of birds fluttering and swooping over the ocean. The trades, diverted by the land masses, headed us more and more as the day progressed. The waves were diverted also. They had been on our starboard quarter, now they swung around to our port side; first the port quarter and then, toward midday, almost broadside to us. They were steeper too, an indication of the raising of the ocean bed. Some burst clear along the ship, drenching the helmsman.

We had hoped for a clear view of the islands some distance off, but by noon our visibility was cut down to perhaps four miles by cloud masses and I could get only a snapshot of the sun which put us thirty miles off the west end of the island of Maui. But Maui was hidden. We could only see masses of clouds, and the squalls now brought heavy rains.

Something odd also happened to *Rainbird*. At the noon roundup *Laymore* was unable to contact her, though we knew she could not be more than a few miles from us. *Laymore* asked us to call her and ask her to relay her position through us. We raised *Rainbird* without trouble and found that during the night she had crossed our course and was now so close in to Maui that the land mass cut her off by radio from *Laymore*.

We were closing rapidly with the land ourselves, but due to the thick weather, visibility was only three miles. All day we peered ahead, looking for land without reward. Then at four in the afternoon, Kevin sighted land fine on our starboard bow. Through the gray of the cloud there ran a faint, steady, sloping line, coming down from the heights to a few hundred feet above sea level where it was smothered in a bank of lowlying cloud.

Land it was, without the slightest shadow of a doubt. There was only one thing wrong with it—it lay on our starboard bow. If this was Haleakala, the big volcano on the east end of Maui, it should have been on our port bow.

I looked at it long and earnestly. I knew the slope. I had studied it with equal care the year before and from the same boat. It was Haleakala and we should bear off. The wind had been veering more and more to the south so that we were now close-hauled and smashing into a steep chop. Perhaps that in itself was an argument in favor of pronouncing the mountain Haleakala and bearing off. For bear off we did, becoming immediately far more comfortable. And two hours and twelve miles later, the murk lifted to show ahead not just a single slope of one side of a mountain, but the whole mountain from sea to peak and sea again. And that mountain was not Haleakala, nor was it Maui.

What island could it be—Oahu? Heavens, was my navigation so bad that we were to lose a chance at second place by coming in on Oahu instead of Maui?

"Molokai," said Kevin.

As he said it, the clouds closed in and the whole island disappeared. It was six in the evening, and the end of the tropical day. There was nothing to guide us, not even a sun shot, and unless I could positively establish my position I could spend hours covering the last twenty or thirty miles to the finish line.

There is a point in ocean-passage making when navigation leaves off and piloting takes over. That point is reached when land is sighted.

We had sighted land, unidentified. It had disappeared. And we had no sun to give a line of position. We had to proceed on dead reckoning from our last known position. One thing I knew we ought to do. We ought to haul close to the wind; for if we ran downwind of Maui now, we would forfeit all our hopes of making any kind of show.

In came the main and in came the Genoa and *Cu Na Mara* became a sort of submarine, hard pressed, her decks awash, flinging seas into the belly of her Genoa. We were at the end of our race and had reached the hardest part of it. And we were in an agony of uncertainty about what island lay ahead. Every hour, every minute was vital now with

*Rainbird* also racing for the finish line somewhere in the murk.

The seas were short and steep, the wind shrill and increasing. Thirty knots, I think, the wind was and, of course, faster than that in the gusts. On we plunged and then, in the lees of the day, Dan and Kevin sighted the end of an island under our starboard. I took a quick bearing on it. A course of 160 magnetic would take us clear of it and to windward. George pronounced the island Molokai in a kind of desperation, and Dan agreed with him. Kevin said he thought it was Molokai. And I said to myself that if it were not Molokai then there was no justice in the world.

I asked Dan to check our last position carefully and draw from it the course we had taken since noon and when he had done this he came to me, at the wheel, and said, "Molokai, Skipper. No mistake." So we held on, fighting to windward in the rising blow, waiting to get into the lee and run down the channel between Molokai and Maui, and pass the finish line—something which seemed, at that time, entirely visionary.

An hour after getting that bearing on the island (which was immediately once again swallowed in clouds) a few lights appeared to port. The seas abated a little but not the wind, which, if anything, was heavier. A little while more and there were lights to port, a dark area dead ahead of us, and lights to starboard, fine on the bow.

Nothing simpler to read than that. The lights to port were those on the end of Maui. The dark area ahead was the channel between Maui and Molokai. The lights fine on the starboard bow were those on the island of Lanai. I so announced to my crew and held my course, being now at the wheel, for in closing with the land I like to do my own steering.

George, however, decided to check. We had aboard an aid to navigation in which I put very little faith—a radio direction finder. He fiddled with this and got the radio station at Kahului on Maui. It was fine on the port bow. A little while later he checked again and the radio station was on the starboard bow.

George went below with Dan, Kevin, and Bob and looked over the chart. I had picked a flashing white light out to starboard which I assumed was a light on the end of Molokai.

"You're headed right into the isthmus of Maui, Skipper," said George emerging from the cabin. "That dark area is the unlighted section of the land at the isthmus and the lights you see to starboard are not on Lanai. They are on the west end of Maui."

I gave Dan the wheel, told him to hold his course while I consulted the chart. What convinced me was the radio station. It had definitely shifted its bearing. It should be broad on my port side. Instead it was fine on my starboard bow.

"Gybe her over," I said and went forward with Rob and the others to help get the Genoa across. I had hardly reached the foredeck before a wave caught *Cu Na Mara* under her quarter, swiveled her head upward and to the side and I went flying across the deck backward toward the lifelines. I grabbed with my left hand, clutched a wire halyard, and saved myself from going overboard.

Murphy made one more effort. We passed the white light, found the west end of Maui and rounded it. The wind was steadily increasing. Now it was blowing forty knots and from ahead. Rob took the wheel while the rest of us trimmed sail. But when we got sail trimmed we found that *Cu Na Mara* was running right for the shore and would not fall off although Rob had the wheel all the way over. We could hear now the mutter of a reef a quarter of a mile off and were making seven knots toward it. The helm would not answer.

There was nothing to do but to drop the Genoa. I went forward with the others to get the Genoa down and in coming back, *Cu Na Mara* jerked viciously once more. Once again I reached out to save myself. This time I grabbed the cockpit coaming, broke two fingers and came down on my knee on the Genoa winch raising a bump as big as a potato.

But that was the end of Murphy. The wind lightened when we were truly around the corner; the sea flattened out to nothing and we marveled at how steady the boat was, and how quietly and easily she slipped through the water, and how soft the night wind was on our salted hides.

We raised the Genoa again and from the land we got scents of earth and of growth so strong that they gripped our throats—the smell of burning sugar cane and of ginger and of the lovely white plumeria. We who, but a few days before, had seen a waterfall in the sky now watched the lighted motor cars gliding along a coastal highway and heard doors slam and dogs bark.

My crew went forward to yarn together in whispers, leaving me at the wheel. We passed a white light to port and a rocket hissed into the air, and there was a cheer from shore.

We had crossed the line and finished the race.

# *Chapter Twenty*

WE HADN'T DONE too badly. On corrected time, we were second in our class and sixth overall out of a fleet of fourteen yachts. We beat *Rainbird* by two hours on corrected time although boat for boat she finished some hours ahead of us. That is worth noting because *Rainbird* is a schooner, modeled after a Gloucester fishermen, and schooners are not supposed to be able to compete with modern racing sloops. She competed very well indeed, and no doubt she had her own share of bad luck.

The big prizes went to F. R. Killam in his lovely *Porpoise III*. He outwitted the weather by sailing north and west of the high and took first overall on elapsed time, first overall on corrected time, the Governor of Hawaii Trophy, and the Province of British Columbia Trophy—a clean sweep of the big awards.

D. D. Nielsen, in his Cal 40, *Moonglow III,* achieved the City of Victoria Trophy for first on elapsed time in his class, and the Founders Trophy for first on corrected time in his class. P. T. Cote in *Jeunesse,* finishing almost two and a half days ahead of *Cu Na Mara,* won the Blue Gavel Club Trophy for first in elapsed time in Division III and the County of Maui Trophy for first on corrected time.

*Cu Na Mara* got a very handsome monkeypod bowl with a plaque for second place on corrected time in Division III.

We were given the warmest of welcomes when we reached Lahaina. Each boat was adopted by a family in Maui—following the excellent tradition of the Transpac, and we were fortunate to have as our patrons Mr. and Mrs. Hugh B. Coates. They came out to meet us in their cabin cruiser *Cadi IV* and as soon as we had crossed the finish line gave us a rousing cheer and pulled alongside.

"Got something for you here," Mr. Coates shouted and swung a pillowslip aboard. And in that pillowslip were three huge bottles of ice-cold champagne.

It was a splendid heartwarming welcome, with flowers and wine and new friends ashore, and later Mr. Coates turned over to us his lovely house so that the first night we slept in proper beds undisturbed by the ship's clock striking the hours of the watch and a shout from the cockpit to relieve the wheel. The Lahaina Yacht Club under Commodore Pat Ballenger, who had been co-sponsors of the race with the Royal Vancouver Yacht Club, put on a special luau for us late arrivals and made us honorary members of the club. Then came the day when it was time to come down out of the clouds and get back to work.

Dan had had to fly back to Seattle immediately after the race. George, Bob, Rob, and Kevin stayed on in Lahaina for a while. I had to return to my home in California. When I sat down at last at my desk there, it was to find the Sears Roebuck catalog open at the pages listing that golf equipment.

I flung the catalog into the wastepaper basket.

Not counting the cost of the boat itself, I figure my second-place prize cost me around five thousand dollars. But you are quite right, Commodore Vanderbilt. A mere trifle. How else could you get so much fun, so much zest and adventure and friendship?

There's a race, they tell me, from Rhode Island to Ireland soon, and it's time indeed that I set foot in Holy Ireland again....